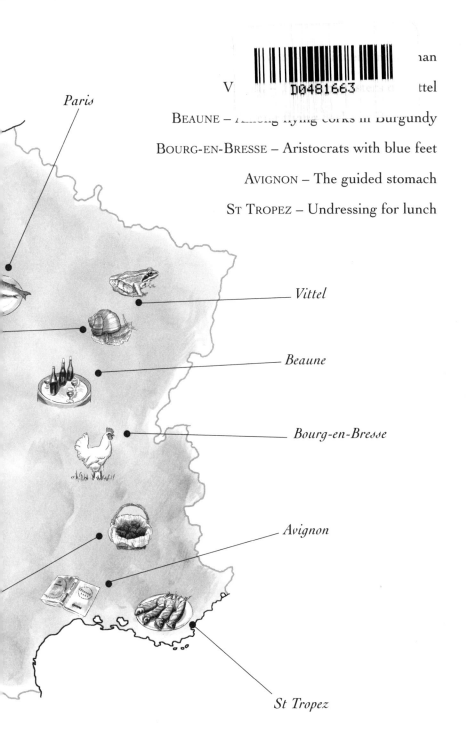

Paris

ıan

V.   ttel

Beaune – *Among flying corks in Burgundy*

Bourg-en-Bresse – Aristocrats with blue feet

Avignon – The guided stomach

St Tropez – Undressing for lunch

Vittel

Beaune

Bourg-en-Bresse

Avignon

St Tropez

Bon appétit!

Also by Peter Mayle

A Year in Provence
Toujours Provence
Hotel Pastis
A Dog's Life
Anything Considered
Chasing Cézanne

Bon appétit!

PETER MAYLE

LITTLE, BROWN AND COMPANY

A *Little, Brown* Book

First published in Great Britain in 2001
by Little, Brown and Company

A CIP catalogue record for this book
is available from the British Library.

ISBN 0 316 85702 5

Typeset in Berkeley by M Rules
Printed and bound in Great Britain by
Clays Ltd, St Ives plc

Little, Brown and Company (UK)
Brettenham House
Lancaster Place
London WC2E 7EN

www.littlebrown.co.uk

Contents

Hors d'oeuvre   1

The inner Frenchman   3

For what we are about to receive   22

Rendezvous in a muddy field   41

The thigh-tasters of Vittel   46

Slow food   69

Undressing for lunch   89

Love at first sniff   107

A connoisseur's marathon   128

Among flying corks in Burgundy   147

Aristocrats with blue feet   167

The guided stomach   190

A civilized purge   208

Last course   230

For Jennie

Hors d'oeuvre

THE PREPARATION OF this book has been an education, made possible by the help of many people. While I can't really thank them adequately, I would like to record my great gratitude to the kind souls who were so patient with my questions, so generous with their time and knowledge, and so hospitable.

In particular, Yves Rousset-Rouard, who took me under his wing during the truffle Mass at Richerenches; Marcel

Loisant, the frog king of Vittel; the Lauzannes, who made me feel truly at home in Normandy; the Beuttlers, my friends and guides in St Tropez; Sylvie Cazes-Régimbeau at Pichon Longueville; Jean-Louis Laville and René Jacqueson in Burgundy; Régis and Sadler, two trusty companions with world-class appetites; and Alain Arnaud, the guardian of Michelin's secrets. To them all, *un très grand merci*.

My thanks also to Ailie Collins, who did her invaluable best to make sure that I was in the right places at the right times.

I can't pretend to have done more than scratch the surface of French gastronomy. But it has been an endlessly interesting, rewarding and enjoyable scratch, even if I never made it to the turkey fair, the cabbage festival or the homage to the herring. Perhaps next time.

1

The inner Frenchman

The early part of my life was spent in the gastronomic wilderness of post-war England, when delicacies of the table were in extremely short supply. I suppose I must have possessed taste buds in my youth, but they were left undisturbed. Food was fuel, and in many cases not very appetizing fuel. I still have vivid memories of boarding school cuisine, which seemed to have been carefully colour-coordinated – grey meat, grey potatoes, grey vegetables, grey flavour. At the time, I thought it was perfectly normal.

I was in for a pleasant shock. Not long after I became the lowliest trainee in an enormous multinational corporation, I was instructed to accompany my first boss, Mr Jenkins, on a trip to Paris as his junior appendage. This was the way, so I was told, to start learning the ropes of big business. I should count myself lucky to have such an opportunity at the tender age of nineteen.

Jenkins was English and proud of it, English to the point of caricature, a role that I think he took some pleasure in cultivating. When going abroad, he announced his nationality and armed himself against the elements with a bowler hat and a strictly furled umbrella. On this occasion, I was his personal bearer, and had been given the important task of carrying his briefcase.

Before we left for the great unknown on the other side of the English Channel, Jenkins had been kind enough to give me some tips on dealing with the natives. One piece of advice was a model of clarity: I should never attempt to get involved with what he referred to as 'their lingo'. Speak English forcefully enough, he said, and they will eventually understand you. When in doubt, shout. It was a simple formula that Jenkins claimed had worked in outposts of the British Empire for hundreds of years, and he saw no reason for changing it now.

Like many of his generation, he had very little good to say about the French – an odd lot who couldn't even understand cricket. But he did admit that they knew their way around a kitchen, and one day he was graciously pleased to accept an invitation from two of his Parisian colleagues to have lunch; or, as Jenkins said, a spot of grub. It was the first memorable meal of my life.

We were taken to a suitably English address, the Avenue Georges V, where there was (and still is) a restaurant called Marius and Janette. Even before sitting down, I could tell I was in a serious establishment, unlike anywhere I'd been before. It smelt different: exotic and tantalizing. There was the scent of the sea as we passed the display of oysters on their bed of crushed ice, the rich whiff of butter warming in a pan, and, coming through the air every time the kitchen door swung open, the pervasive – and to my untravelled nose, infinitely foreign – hum of garlic.

Jenkins surrendered his hat and umbrella as we sat down, and I looked with bewilderment at the crystal forest of glasses and the armoury of knives and forks laid out in front of me. The trick was to start on the outside and work inwards, so I was told. But the correct choice of cutlery was a minor problem compared to making sense of the elaborate mysteries described on the pages of the menu. What was a *bar grillé*? What was a *loup à l'écaille*? And what in heaven's name was *aioli*? All I had to help me was schoolboy French, and I hadn't been a particularly gifted schoolboy. I dithered over these puzzling choices in a fog of almost complete ignorance, too timid to ask for help.

Jenkins, quite unconsciously, came to my rescue. 'Personally,' he said, 'I never eat anything I can't pronounce.' He closed his menu with a decisive snap. 'Fish and chips for me. They do a very decent fish and chips in France. Not quite like ours, of course.'

With a sense of relief, I said I'd have the same. Our two French colleagues raised four surprised eyebrows. No oysters to start with? No *soupe de poissons*? The company was paying; there was no need to hold back. But Jenkins was adamant. He couldn't abide the texture of oysters – 'slippery little blighters' was how he described them – and he didn't care for the way soup had a tendency to cling to his moustache. Fish and chips would suit him very nicely, thank you.

By this time, I was already enjoying a minor revelation, which was the bread. It was light and crusty and slightly chewy, and I spread on to it some of the pale, almost white butter from the slab on a saucer in front of me. A slab. English butter in those days was highly salted and a lurid shade of yellow, and it was doled out in small, grudging pats. At the first mouthful of French bread and French butter, my taste buds, dormant until then, went into spasm.

The fish, a majestic creature that I think was sea bass, was ceremoniously presented, filleted in seconds with a spoon and fork, and arranged with great care on my plate. My previous experience of fish had been limited to either cod or plaice, heavily disguised, in accordance with English preference, under a thick shroud of batter. In contrast, the sea bass, white and fragrant with what I now know was fennel, looked curiously naked. It was all very strange.

Even the chips, the *pommes frites*, didn't resemble the sturdy English variety. These chips, a golden pyramid of them served on a separate dish, were pencil-slim, crisp between the teeth, tender to chew, a perfect foil for the delicate flesh of the fish. It was lucky for me that I wasn't required to contribute to the conversation of my elders and betters; I was too busy discovering real food.

Then there was cheese. Or rather, there were a dozen or more cheeses, another source of confusion after years of having only the simple choice of Cheddar or Gorgonzola. I thought I recognized a vaguely familiar shape, safe and Cheddar-like, and pointed to it. The waiter insisted on giving me two other cheeses as well, so that I could compare the textural delights of hard, medium, and creamy. More of that bread. More signals of joy from the taste buds, which were making up for lost time.

Tarte aux pommes. Even I knew what that was; even Jenkins knew. 'Excellent,' he said. 'Apple pie. I wonder if they have any proper cream.' Unlike the apple pies of my youth, with a

thick crust top and bottom, the tart on my plate was topless, displaying the fruit – wafers of apple, beautifully arranged in overlapping layers, glistening with glaze on a sliver of buttery pastry.

Too young to be offered an expense-account cigar and a

balloon of brandy, I sat in a daze of repletion while my companions puffed away and considered a return to the cares of office. I was slightly tipsy after my two permitted glasses of wine, and I completely forgot that I was responsible for the all-important Jenkins briefcase. When we left the restaurant, I left it under the table, which demonstrated to him that I was not executive material, and which marked the beginning of the end of my career in that particular company. But, much more important, lunch had been a personal turning point, the loss of my gastronomic virginity.

It wasn't only because of what I had eaten, although that had been incomparably better than anything I'd eaten before. It was the total experience: the elegance of the table setting, the ritual of opening and tasting the wine, the unobtrusive efficiency of the waiters and their attention to detail, arranging the plates just so, whisking up bread crumbs from the tablecloth. For me, it had been a special occasion. I couldn't imagine people eating like this every day; and yet, in France, they did. It was the start of an enduring fascination with the French and their love affair with food.

It is, of course, the most whiskery old cliché, but clichés

usually have their basis in fact, and this one certainly does. Historically, the French have paid extraordinary – some would say excessive – attention to what they eat and how they eat it. And they put their money where their mouth is, spending a greater proportion of their income on food and drink than any other nation in the world. This is true not only of the affluent bourgeois gourmet; where food is concerned, interest, enjoyment, and knowledge extend throughout all levels of society, from the President to the peasant.

Nature must take some of the credit for this. If you were to make a list of the ideal conditions for agriculture, livestock and game, seafood and wine, you would find that most of them exist in one part or another of France. Fertile soil, varied climate, the fishing grounds of the Channel, the Atlantic and the Mediterranean – every natural advantage is here except for a tropical region. (Although, such is the luck of the French, they have Guadeloupe and Martinique to provide them with rum and coconuts.) Living in the middle of such abundance, it's not surprising that the Frenchman makes the most of it.

The other major national gastronomic asset is an army of outstanding chefs, and for this the French have to give some credit to one of the more grisly periods in their history. Before their Revolution, the best cooking was not available to the general public. The most talented chefs sweated over their hot stoves in private for their aristocratic masters, creating multi-course banquets in the kitchens of mansions and palaces. And then, in 1789, the guillotine struck. The aristocracy more or less disappeared, and so did their private kitchens. Faced with the prospect of having nobody to cook for and nowhere to cook, many of the unemployed chefs did the intelligent and democratic thing: they opened restaurants and began to cook for their fellow citizens. The common man could now enjoy the food of kings, prepared by the finest chefs in France. *Liberté, égalité, gastronomie.*

More than two hundred years later, the common man still does pretty well, despite what pessimists will tell you about times changing for the worse. It's true that traditions are under attack from several directions. For a start, more than 50 per cent of all food bought in France is now provided by supermarkets rather than small specialty stores. (A statistic that doesn't seem to apply to those faithful Parisians who line up every day outside the Poilane bakery in the Rue du Cherche-Midi. I've bought bread there several times, and the wait has never been less than ten minutes.) Then there is television, eating into mealtimes and often competing successfully with a proper dinner. And *le fast food* is working its insidiously convenient spell, with Big Macs on the Champs Élysées and pizza stands in every town market. All in all, the future of traditional French cuisine, with its hours of shopping, preparing, and cooking, followed by further hours of eating, doesn't look too promising; not, at least, if you believe some of the gloomy predictions made by those wise men who claim to see the writing on the kitchen wall.

I am more optimistic, perhaps because I tend to compare France with other countries instead of comparing the France of today with the France of yesterday, with all the rosy distortions of nostalgia. At any rate, I see encouraging signs that some traditions are healthier than ever, and that gastronomy is holding its own against what Régis, my friend the glutton-in-chief, calls 'industrial food'. Here are just a few examples.

The star chefs, men like Ducasse and Guérard and Bras and Troisgros, enjoy a level of celebrity and popular prestige reserved in other countries for the gods of sport and television. If any of them were to open a new restaurant, it would be national news. If, God forbid, their standards should ever slip, it would be a national catastrophe, a *tremblement de terre*, an earthquake, probably marked by sorrowful editorials in *Le Monde* and *Le Figaro*. And the clients of these top chefs are not all millionaires, cabinet ministers, or expense-account cowboys. Monsieur Dupont, the average Frenchman, is prepared to invest in his stomach, saving up to eat at the best restaurants, often travelling considerable distances to do so. But, to borrow a phrase from the Michelin guide, *ça vaut le voyage*. It's worth the trip.

One can say the same about more modest restaurants with lesser-known chefs. Some of them can be found in the back streets of provincial towns, like L'Isle Sonnante in Avignon: small, charming, and delicious. Others are buried so deeply in the countryside that you might think their only clients would be the local postman and his wife, or travellers who had lost their way, something that happened to me one summer's day a couple of years ago.

I had taken a shortcut – always a bad idea for a geographically challenged person like myself with a severely limited sense of direction – and found myself lost. Even worse, it was lunchtime. It was hot. The back roads into which I'd strayed were deserted. The signposts bore unfamiliar names. I was irritated with myself for not staying in Aix for lunch.

Fate intervened. I had stopped at a fork in the road. Chance made me turn right instead of left, and two minutes later, I arrived in the miniature village of Saint Martin de la Brasque. It was a sight to restore one's faith in shortcuts. There was a tiny square; the houses on it had their windows shuttered against the heat. Tables and chairs were set out in the shade cast by a line of plane trees, and lunch was being served. The air was so still I could hear the splash of the village fountain, one of the best of all summer sounds. I was delighted that I hadn't stayed in Aix.

I don't remember exactly what I ate that first time under the trees at the Restaurant de la Fontaine, but I do remember thinking that the food was like the most satisfying kind of home cooking: simple, generous, and tasty. I was given a table next to the fountain, an arm's length from the wine keeping cool in the water. Madame Girand, the young proprietor, told me that her husband was the chef, and that the restaurant stayed open throughout the year.

Since then, I've been back many times. The food has always been good and the restaurant has nearly always been well attended, even in winter. Word has spread. People come from as far away as Aix, or from the other side of the Luberon, an hour or more by car. *Ça vaut le voyage.*

If Madame Girand and her husband have the stamina to keep at it for the next thirty or forty years, La Fontaine might join those other restaurants, large and small, that have become institutions. You find them all over France, places like Chez L'Ami Louis in Paris or the Auberge in La Mole. They are not always the most fashionable of restaurants, nor are they the most eulogized by the guide books. But they have something about them that I – not to mention a few hundred thousand French customers – find irresistible; a very distinct character, the comforting feeling that you and your appetite couldn't possibly be in better hands.

There is an air of confidence about these restaurants that comes from three or four decades of practice. They know what they do best, and they do it, ignoring the fads of the day. Their menus will be adjusted, but only slightly, to reflect the seasons. Asparagus will appear in the spring, wild mushrooms in the fall, truffles in the winter. As for the rest – the scallops, the terrines, the lamb, the *confits*, the *gratins* of potatoes, the *tartes maison* and *crèmes brûlées* – why ever think of changing them? They are the classics that have kept generations of people happy.

Naturally, the food and wine in these establishments will be brought to your table by that most excellent and highly skilled of men, the professional waiter. There seems to be a widely held belief nowadays that anyone who has enough physical coordination to balance a tray on the palm of one hand has what it takes to be a waiter. It is something young people often do while they're deciding what to do. Usually amiable and eager to please, but very seldom knowledgeable, they provide little more than a transport service between kitchen and customer. A serious waiter, a career waiter, is in

a different league. He can add another layer of enjoyment to
your meal.

You should ask him to be your guide, because he knows
the food better than you do. He himself has probably eaten
everything on the menu dozens of times over the past twenty
years. He can tell you exactly how each dish is cooked and
what would be the ideal combination of courses, light and
heavy, savoury and sweet. And he is on close personal terms
with the cellar, particularly with some small local wines that
you may not have come across before.

Now watch him at work. It seems effortless. There is no
furtive wrestling with the wine bottle; the cork never sticks or
breaks, but comes out with a smooth turn of the wrist, to be
given a brief, considered sniff of approval. Nothing is rushed,
and yet all you need – *cornichons* to go with the pâté, or a
good fierce mustard for the *daube* – is there on your table
when it should be. The bread basket is refilled, the glasses are
topped up. You don't have to ask for anything. Your man is
telepathic. He knows what you need before you know it yourself.

I'm sure that waiters like this exist in other countries, but
in France there seem to be so many of them – unhurried,
calm, on top of their job. It is considered an honourable occupation. I like that. In fact, I have often thought that these
superlative waiters deserve some official recognition, and
there could be no better place for them to receive it than in
the pages of another flourishing French institution, the
Michelin guide.

The guide celebrated its one hundredth birthday in 2000. It

was published, as usual, in March – a red-covered tome, bulging with good addresses and, as usual, it flew off bookstore shelves. Other countries, of course, have their restaurant guides (considerably slimmer than the Michelin), and some of them do very well. But the Michelin does better than very well; it is an immediate national best-seller, year after year. In a later chapter, we shall see some of the discreet workings of the red guide in more detail. I only mention it here because it is another example of a thriving gastronomic tradition, and of the continuing search for exceptional food in every corner of the country.

Where else would people get worked up about salt? To the rest of the world, salt is a necessary but anonymous part of the diet, about as fascinating as a glass of tap water. But not in France. Here, salt is something that gourmets argue about. Some of them will tell you that the ultimate saline experience is *sel de Guérande*, the grey, crystallized sea salt gathered along the Brittany coast; others prefer the white *Fleur de Sel* found in the Camargue. Not long ago, I bought some to try. It came in a decorative cork-topped pot, and the label featured the name – in this case Christian Carrel from Aigues-Mortes – of the *saunier* who gathered the salt. Very good it is too, particularly when sprinkled on radishes or fresh tomatoes.

More and more small companies, or individuals like Carrel, are making visible efforts through their labels and packaging to separate themselves from the industrial food business. The chicken farmers of Bresse have been doing it for years; every single bird wears on one ankle an aluminium identification ring, marked with the farmer's name and address. Now you

can find similar detailed information – with its implicit promise
of higher quality – on jams and *tapenades* and cheeses, on
sausage and olive oil and honey and *pastis*. These delicacies
are likely to cost more than their mass-produced competitors.
But the difference in taste is worth the difference in price.

More proof that the French stomach is far from being
neglected is spread out in front of you every week at any one
of a thousand markets throughout the country. In Provence
alone, there are enough of them to offer you the choice of a
different market every day, and they seem to be in no danger
of suffering from lack of customers. On the contrary, they
appear to be getting bigger and more popular. I remember
Coustellet market twenty years ago, when there were no more
than ten or twelve small vans in the village parking area. You
could buy local vegetables and fruit, some goat cheese, half a
dozen eggs, and that was just about it. Today, the market has
grown until it covers nearly an acre, and in high season it's
packed every Sunday morning.

It's not only what the French eat that sets them apart from
so many other nationalities, but how they eat it. They concentrate on their food, sometimes to such an extent that they
put aside the joys of arguing with one another. And they are
determined to extract the last ounce of pleasure from a meal,
a tendency that my old boss Mr Jenkins liked to describe as
'making beasts of themselves'.

There is a wonderful photograph taken, I think, in the
1920s, that shows a group of men in suits seated around a
table. They are about to eat spit-roasted *ortolans* – tiny, lark-
like birds that are now a protected species. But before taking

that first crunchy mouthful, they must observe the ritual of appreciating the bouquet. This is the moment that has been captured by the photographer. There they sit, these respectable, well-dressed men, each of them bent low over his plate, with his head completely covered by a napkin, so that the fragrant steam can be trapped, inhaled, and properly savoured. It looks for all the world like a coven of the Ku Klux Klan saying grace before having lunch.

No doubt when the *ortolans* are finished there will be a little sauce or gravy remaining on the plate. Too exquisite to leave, this final treat will have to be dealt with in the correct manner, using a piece of purpose-built cutlery that only a Frenchman could have invented. It resembles a spoon that has been flattened, leaving no more than the hint of a lip along one side. The sole function of this ingenious utensil is to scoop up what is left of the sauce in a genteel fashion, thus avoiding the plebeian habit – one that I love – of using bread as a mop.

As it happens, there is a socially acceptable way to do even this if the cutlery doesn't run to a full set of equipment. You take your bread, tear it up into small pieces, and then use your knife and fork to steer the bread through the sauce until you have cleaned your plate. I learned this at a dinner party some years ago, where my host was delighted to instruct me on some of the differences between English and French table etiquette; and, of course, the superiority of the French way of doing things.

As a boy, I was taught to keep my hands under the table when they were not occupied with knife or fork or glass, a curious habit, my host said, and one that encourages mischievous behaviour. It is well known that hands at English dinner parties have a tendency to wander under the table, squeezing a thigh, caressing a knee, and generally getting up to no good. In the best French households, the rule is the reverse: idle hands must be kept on the table. Dalliance cannot be allowed to interfere with food. First things first is the rule, and, during dinner at least, fondling is prohibited.

Hastily putting my hands back where they should be, I asked if there were a logical reason why the French, unlike the Anglo-Saxons, almost always set the table with the forks facing downward. Was it, I wondered, to protect tender and well-brought-up fingers from being pricked by the tines of the fork? My host looked at me with an expression I've seen a hundred times before on a hundred French faces – half-amused, half-puzzled. How could I be so ignorant about something so obvious? Forks are placed like that, of course, in order to display the family crest engraved on the back.

Learning about food – learning to eat – is a series of edible adventures and surprises. For instance, just when you think you have mastered the potato, that such a basic ingredient could have nothing new to offer, you discover *aligot*, a velvety blend of mashed potatoes, garlic, and Cantal cheese. Or you are introduced to the unlikely but triumphant combination of tiny wild strawberries served not with cream, but with vinaigrette sauce. Then you encounter roasted figs. The education of the stomach never ends.

And it is normally a most pleasant process. The people who spend their lives making good things to eat and drink are, on the whole, a very congenial bunch, pleased when you show an interest in their work and more than happy to explain how they do it. I have occasionally seen chefs frazzled and bad-tempered at the end of a fourteen-hour working day, and I remember one chef who was so terminally drunk that he fell backwards out of his kitchen, cursing loudly. But these were exceptions. On the whole, working with food and wine seems to bring out the better side of human nature. It's difficult to imagine a misanthrope who is prepared to spend his days doing something that gives so much pleasure to others.

Enjoyment is contagious, and this is perhaps best experienced during one particular meal of the week. Here you will see children, parents, grandparents and occasionally the family dog; young couples giving themselves a treat; elderly ladies and gentlemen poring over the menu as if the pages held the secret of life; local families dressed to kill, and visiting Parisians decked out in full rural chic – a mixture of generations and social backgrounds, gathered together to observe another tradition that shows no sign of dying out: Sunday lunch.

For me, there is one moment in particular that almost makes the meal by itself. Aperitifs have been served – *pastis* or *kir* or white wine or, on red-letter days, champagne – and menus are being read with the concentration of a lawyer going through a page of fine print. Suggestions and counter-suggestions go back and forth across the tables. The carpaccio of fresh tuna? The *soupe au pistou*? The asparagus flan? And then what? The cod in a herb crust? The stew of veal and peppers? *Or pieds et paquets*, the Provençal recipe that elevates humble mutton tripe to new heights?

In fact, it doesn't matter what you choose. It is those few moments of anticipatory limbo that are special. For five or ten minutes, conversations are muted, gossip and family matters are put aside, and everyone in the restaurant is mentally tasting the dishes on offer. You can almost hear the flutter of taste buds.

Lunch progresses at an unhurried pace, as all good lunches should. People eat more slowly on Sundays, and drink a little more wine than usual. They forget to look at their watches. Two hours slip by, often more. Eventually, with appetites satisfied, a drowsy calm comes over the room as the plates are cleared away, the tablecloths are brushed, and coffee is served. A lazy afternoon lies ahead: a book, a doze, a swim. The chef makes a ceremonial tour of the tables, gathering compliments, happy to share with you one or two favourite recipes. Curiously, these dishes never taste quite the same at home, no matter how carefully the recipe is followed, no matter how talented the cook. There is something about Sunday lunch in a French country restaurant that goes beyond food. But unfortunately, ambience doesn't travel.

In the course of preparing this book – those long hours with knife and fork and glass that I like to call research – I was surprised by two things. The first was the high level of enthusiasm for any event, however bizarre, that sought to turn eating and drinking into a celebration. The amount of effort put in by the organizers, the stallholders and the general public (who, in some cases, had travelled halfway across France) was astonishing. I cannot imagine any other race prepared to devote an entire weekend to frogs' legs or snails or the critical assessment of chickens.

And while the French take their passions seriously, my second surprise was to discover that those of them who come to these events don't take themselves seriously at all. They dress up in outlandish costumes. They sing the most unexpected songs – 'It's A Long Way To Tipperary' being just one – at the top of their voices and often wildly off-key. They make fun of one another, eat and drink like champions, and generally let their hair down. Not at all what one might expect from a nation with a reputation for reserved and slightly chilly good manners.

For many years, there has been a saying in England that I imagine must reflect a widely held view: 'Lovely country, France. Pity about the French.' Perhaps I've been lucky. All the French I met on my travels were helpful, good-natured and sometimes embarrassingly generous. There were the strangers who invited me to stay at their home when there was no room at the local hotel, the farmer who presented me with a bottle of 1935 Calvados made by his grandfather, and dozens of others who went out of their way to make sure I had as good a time as they were having.

I hope I've done them justice in the pages that follow. To all of them, thanks for the memories.

2

For what we are about to receive

Twenty-first century France is not a country in which one feels an overwhelming sense of religion. There are, to be sure, saints' days by the hundred, each one recorded in the official post office calendar. There are patron saints keeping a protective eye on everything from villages and vegetables to farmers and carpenters (although I've looked in vain in the hope of finding the patron saint of writers). There is, tucked away with the weather forecast in the local newspaper, *le saint du jour*, whose name appears beneath an illustration of an angel blowing a trumpet. There are magnificent cathedrals, abbeys, and convents. There are churches of every age and size. There are also, in many of those stately properties snoozing away the centuries behind high stone walls, private chapels. Places of worship are everywhere. But most of them, most of the time, are empty. Only a handful of the French population – one recent estimate puts it at 10 per cent – goes to church on a regular basis.

'The fact of it is,' said Monsieur Farigoule, the retired schoolmaster who gives regular dissertations from his perch by the village bar on the worsening state of the world, 'the plain fact of it is that the religion of the French is food. And wine, of course.' He tapped his empty glass with a fingernail to indicate that he might be persuaded to accept a refill. 'We worship the belly, and our high priests are chefs. We would rather sit and eat than kneel and pray. It pains me to say such things about my countrymen, but patriotic sentiment cannot be allowed to hide the truth.'

He drew himself up to his full height, such as it is, a fraction over five feet, and glared at me, clearly anticipating an argument. He has never forgotten a minor difference of opinion we once had over the tactics of the English rugby team – Farigoule accused them of biting their opponents' ears in the scrum – and he considers me a dissident, a potential troublemaker. This is a distinction I have in common with everyone else who doesn't share his views. The great Farigoule is, by his own admission, never wrong.

In this case, I happened to agree with him. You don't have

to be particularly observant to notice that restaurants in France consistently attract larger audiences than churches, and I said so.

At that, Farigoule pounced. '*Eh alors?*' he said. He cocked his head and nodded encouragingly, the patient professor trying to coax an answer from a terminally dim student. 'How do you explain this? What could be the reason, do you think?'

'Well,' I said, 'for one thing, the food's better . . .'

'*Bof!*' He delivered his most withering look, holding up both hands to ward off any further heresy. 'Why do I waste my time with intellectual pygmies?'

He was on potentially dangerous ground with pygmies, given his height, only slightly enhanced by thick crepe-soled shoes, but I resisted the urge to comment. 'As it happens,' I said, 'I'm going to church myself on Sunday.'

'*You?*' Farigoule's eyebrows almost took off from his head.

'Certainly. Morning Mass. No doubt I'll see you there.' And with that, I escaped before he could start asking awkward questions.

I was indeed going to church, but I couldn't pretend that it was entirely for religious or even social reasons. The decision to go had been inspired by food. This, in Farigoule's eyes, would be yet another nail in the coffin containing my deplorable character; it would confirm my moral turpitude, gluttony, and general worthlessness. So I wasn't about to give him the satisfaction of knowing that I was going to attend the annual *messe des truffes* in Richerenches, a village north-east of Orange. This was to be a sacred event, under the patronage

of Saint Antoine, at which thanks would be given for the aromatic, mysterious, and breathtakingly expensive black truffle.
What's more, such are the blessings that reward the devout,
there would be lunch after the service. A lunch that included
truffles.

I had been told to arrive early if I wanted to be sure of a
place in the church, and it was just after 7 a.m. when I left the
warmth of our kitchen and flinched at the bitterly cold
January drizzle. It was still dark, and it seemed set to be one
of those days – only fifty-two of them a year, according to
local mythology – when the sun wasn't going to shine over
Provence.

Dawn made a halfhearted attempt to break through the
murk, but there was nothing even an optimist could call light
until I left the autoroute at Bollene and turned east on one of
the minor roads leading to Richerenches. This is wine country, and as gloom gave way to grey I could make out the
twisted, blackened claws of clipped vines stretching away for
miles across the low hills. Trees were crouched low against
the wind. Nothing moved on the landscape. Two disconsolate
magpies, normally the most dapper of birds, were huddled,
heads down, by the side of the road like bedraggled old men
waiting for a bus.

Villages without people appeared through the windscreen
wipers: Suze-la-Rousse, where a university of wine has been
installed in the fourteenth-century chateau; La Baume-de-
Transit, shuttered, dripping, and silent; and then, as the rain
died away after a final flurry of spitting, Richerenches.

The name of the main street provides a whiff of what

preoccupies the village during the winter months: the Avenue de la Rabasse, or Truffle Avenue, is the setting for a truffle market every Saturday morning from November through to March. I had been there once before on market day, making my way slowly along the line of dealers, each with a modest fortune in fungus displayed in small sacks or plastic bags. Feeling like a novice attending an ancient ritual for the first time, I imitated some of the buyers who seemed to have perfected the correct technique. Like them, I bent to inhale the ripe, almost rotten scent coming from the bags. I made admiring comments about the bouquet, about the impressive size and colour and undeniable beauty of the deformed black lumps. And like the others, I was careful to wince in horror at the price per kilo. This information was delivered in a mutter from the corner of the mouth, accompanied by a shrug. *Eh beh oui* – what can you expect? Good ones, like these jewels here, are few and far between, almost impossible to find.

I had explored the original heart of the village behind the market. Richerenches had started life in the twelfth century as a commandery, or fort, built by the Knights Templars. They had followed the classic rectangular plan of military architecture, with stone walls as thick as small rooms, and round towers at each corner. Impregnable for centuries, the fort had now been invaded by pint-sized Peugeots and Citroëns, squeezed into spaces that would have been a tight fit for a well-fed horse.

Low archways led into dark alleys, smelling of history. The houses were small and well kept, intimately close to one another. A single rowdy neighbour could keep the entire village awake. The largest open space was in front of the church, and I went up to try its heavy nailed door. It was locked. On that particular bright Saturday morning, village devotions were taking place over the plastic bags in the market.

This being a special Sunday, things would be different, I was sure, but Richerenches was in no hurry to get up and greet the day. I was the first customer in the café, just as the coffee machine was performing the opening movement in its symphony of hisses and splutters while madame behind the bar flicked a cloth at nonexistent dust.

Early morning in a French country café. The furniture, chosen for function rather than style, is arranged with meticulous precision, a tin ashtray centred on each table, chairs neatly tucked in. The day's edition of the local newspaper, in this case *La Provence*, lies on a ledge inside the door, its pages of regional news smooth and unthumbed. The tiled floor, swabbed down the night before with water and a dab of linseed oil, is still spotless, unsullied by the sugar-cube wrappers and cigarette butts that by the end of each day accumulate in a scuffed row on the floor by the bar. (This is normal. For some inscrutable French reason, ashtrays on café bars are rare, and smokers there are expected to drop their butts on the floor and stub them out by foot.) Bottles gleam on the shelf, practically every variety of brand name alcohol one can imagine, with one or two local curiosities thrown in. There is always a choice of several different kinds of *pastis*, reflecting a thirst for the national nectar that accounts for the consumption of twenty million glasses a day.

The café smell is distinctive, and not to everyone's taste – a mixture of strong coffee and black tobacco, with occasional piercing undertones of bleach. It's a distinctively French smell, which I happen to like, as it reminds me of the many happy hours I've spent being a foreign fly on café walls. The sounds – the clash of cups, the scrape of chairs, the rasp of an early morning cough – echo against the hard surfaces. Then there's a boom, as a second customer comes in and wishes the room a sonorous *bonjour.* He has the massive build to match his big voice, and he is friendly enough to offer me, a solitary stranger, his hand to shake as he passes my table. His palm feels like iced sandpaper. Standing at the bar, he sips coffee from a cup, with his little finger delicately extended. When he pays, it is with change extracted, coin by coin, from a battered leather purse no bigger than a box of matches. Does any other country in the world issue dainty purses to its largest male inhabitants?

More customers arrive, all men, regulars who know one another, and the boom level increases. That morning, in voices that could easily carry to the other end of the village, they condemned the awful weather. There's nothing to be done about it, but perhaps a quick shot of red wine would help, tossed back with a shrug. At least they'd be indoors today, and the church should be warm. Some tourists trickle in. Heads turn in unison to inspect them, then turn back again, like spectators watching a tennis match.

I left the café to find more life on the street, much of it clearly not local. A television crew of fashionably razor-cropped and bestubbled young men was unloading equipment, dodging cars with foreign plates that were nosing around looking for parking spaces. Men and women with smooth pink indoor complexions, wearing elegant foul-weather clothes of Parisian cut, were hovering indecisively on the pavement. It was time to go to church before all the pews were taken.

The rest of the world seemed to have had the same idea. The church doors were not yet open, but the small *place* in front of the steps was packed with truffle worshippers, some more official than others. Moving through the crowd like visitors from another century were senior members of the truffle brotherhood, the Confrérie du Diamant Noir, in full and formal regalia: black cloaks to mid-calf, medals suspended from their necks on yellow and black striped ribbons, wide-brimmed black hats. I watched two of them who had found a space at the edge of the crowd and were comparing truffles taken from hiding places beneath their cloaks. Each showed the other his truffle, cupped in both hands and partly concealed, presumably to prevent curious eyes from catching a glimpse of it. Their heads were tilted, close enough for their hat brims to touch as they whispered to each other. They might have been conspirators exchanging state secrets.

I'd been told to bring a truffle with me, and I checked to make sure that the precious foil-wrapped lump was safe in my pocket. Suddenly, there was the sound of iron grating against iron, followed by the regular hollow clang of the bell, causing alarm and temporary deafness among a flock of pigeons that erupted from the belfry. I felt the pressure of the crowd, like a huge animal, pushing me closer to the steps of the church.

Then the doors were opened. The members of the congregation nudged and jostled their way inside, with as much decorum as they could manage while jockeying for position with a good view close to the altar. The French have never taken to the Anglo-Saxon habit of the orderly queue, which they consider far too inconvenient for everyday use.

The church was warm and bright and in noticeably good condition – the pale stone arches unmarked and smooth, the woodwork polished, fresh flowers arranged around the altar. The choir rustled its hymn sheets and discreetly cleared its throat. A current of air brought a distinctive smell to the nose: not incense, not dust, not even sanctity, but an earthy hint of the reason we were all gathered here. On the lace-trimmed pulpit, set out like a row of arthritic black fists, were six of the largest truffles I'd ever seen, each one a quarter-pounder at least, brushed clean of every speck of mud. It was a sight to warm the cockles of a gourmet's heart.

There was none of the hush you would expect to find before the start of a religious service. Some of my fellow-worshippers might have been keeping their conversations to a whisper, but they were outnumbered by others who were in full voice – calling out to friends, commenting on the flowers, the satisfying magnificence of the truffles, and the size of the crowd, which by now had spilled over on to the steps outside the church. I could hear the clack of camera shutters and the pop of flashbulbs above the buzz of talk as press photographers jostled with the television crew for the best angles.

The arrival of the presiding priest, Père Gleize, brought a semblance of calm. He looked as every man of the church should look – a halo of silver hair, the face of a mature cherub, an expression of good-humoured tranquillity. With a smile of great sweetness, he made us welcome, and the service began.

As the mixture of prayer and singing filled the church with words and music that had hardly changed in a thousand years, the modern world seemed far, far away; that is, as long as you kept your eyes closed. Open them, and there was no doubt that you were in the twenty-first century, although the television crew was trying its hardest to be unobtrusive. Another contemporary touch was displayed by the altar boy, well-scrubbed, fair-haired, and altogether angelic, with the pneumatic snouts of his Sunday best sneakers poking out from the bottom of his traditional white vestments.

The sermon began. Père Gleize had chosen to deliver it in *lengo nostro*, 'our tongue', or Provençal, and to my ignorant ear very little was familiar. It is said there are traces of Latin and Greek to be found in the dialect, but the overall sound is like a more orotund version of French, filled with wonderful rolling words: *escoundoun* and *moulounado* and *cauto-cauto*. Apart from *amen*, there was only one word in the entire sermon I could identify for sure. It was, not surprisingly, *rabasse*, the truffle, and it was making its presence felt more and more strongly throughout the church as collection baskets started going up and down the rows. A basket was passed to the man next to me. He held it in both hands like a chalice, lowered his head, and took a deep sniff before unwrapping the aluminium foil from his own contribution and popping it into the basket with the other truffles.

To encourage us in our giving, the choir performed a chant to Saint Antoine. And he was left in no doubt about what was being asked of him:

> *Bon Saint Antoine, donne-nous*
> *Des truffes en abondance*
> *Que leur odeur et leur bon gout*
> *Fassent aimer la Provence*

In other words, give us truffles. Lots of truffles.

This was not the simple cry of greed that it might appear to be. If Saint Antoine had done his stuff, there would be plenty of truffles in circulation. And the more there were, the more the house of the Lord would benefit, because, following tradition, the truffles collected would be auctioned off after the

service, with all proceeds going to charity and the church.

The donations were taken back to be counted. Those baskets that I could see looked comfortably prosperous, filled with an extravagant salad of truffles and large-denomination bank notes. With God now having been served by Mammon, the congregation rose, and the choir sent us on our way with Handel's 'Hallelujah Chorus'. Outside, the rain had held off – 'divine providence,' I heard one pious old truffler mutter as he looked up at the sky – and the auction could take place as planned in the open air, outside the Hôtel de Ville.

The centre of operations was a table in the square, and with the crowd beginning to gather, the auctioneer climbed up to stand on top. He was one of the *confrères*, a gentleman who would certainly have walked off with the *grand prix* for the most impressive moustache of the day. It was an altogether splendid appendage: luxuriant, with a fine upward gravity-defying curl, its wingspan almost as wide as the brim of his *confrère's* black hat; a virtuoso among moustaches.

Rumours of the day's collection began to pass through the crowd, and the news was not good. Buyers were going to have to dig deeply into their pockets, because the contents of the baskets reflected this year's disappointing crop. There were barely three kilos (not quite seven pounds) of truffles. Last year there had been seven kilos (more than fifteen pounds). Prices would therefore be high. But according to Monsieur Escoffier, the octogenarian *confrère*, it would be money well spent. '*La truffe*,' he was heard to say, '*ça rend les femmes plus gentilles et les hommes plus galants*.' The bonus of kinder women and more gallant men was surely worth a little extra.

Giving each side of his moustache an upward flick with the back of his hand, the auctioneer got down to business. With the aplomb of a veteran from Sotheby's, he prepared his audience for an expensive morning. 'Rain didn't come in the summer when it should have,' he said, 'and so truffles are scarce. Extremely scarce. Now as you all know, the cost of rarity is high. But . . .' he spread his hands, palms up, and shrugged at the crowd '. . . you can always economize on your wine.'

He held up the first truffle for all to see, and a bid of nine hundred francs came from the front of the crowd. The auctioneer peered at the bidder with an expression of scornful amazement. 'Can I believe what I hear? A miserable nine hundred francs? This monster weighs two hundred and twenty grams. And it's spotless, ready for the omelette. Not a trace of earth on it.' He looked down from his elevated position on the table at the faces around him, one hand raised hopefully to his ear. A thousand francs was bid. Not enough. He brought out his secret weapon, a sales incentive Sotheby's would kill for: God was on the side of the auctioneer. 'Do you want to be saved, you band of sinners? Come on! Pay up!' Encouraged by thoughts of salvation, bidders pushed the price to fifteen hundred francs (about £150), and the hammer came down.

The auctioneer's patter continued, liberally sprinkled with references to the Almighty and recipe hints, until the last truffle had been sold. With the cash that had already been donated, the morning's total was announced and greeted with applause: the sum of 24,700 francs had been raised. But the auctioneer, still in the grip of sales fever, hadn't quite finished. One of the empty collection baskets caught his eye and tickled his imagination: 'This is worth a fortune,' he said. 'It's been blessed!' Sure enough, the basket fetched 1,000 francs. The magic figure of 25,000 francs had been passed. One way or another, we had all earned our lunch.

There is nothing like the combination of cold weather and good deeds to sharpen the appetite. And the highlight of the menu being served at the Richerenches village hall was *omelette aux truffes*, an inducement that has never been known to fail in France. Rarely have I seen a crowd move with such speed and purpose, and by the time I looked up again after scribbling a few notes, I had the *place* practically to myself.

The hall was a scene of amiable chaos as everyone moved among the tables looking for their names on slips of paper that identified reservations. I found my place and shook every hand within reach during a blur of introductions. My neighbours were local, jolly, and thirsty.

On occasions like this, I have always found that it is a social advantage to be foreign. Wine is pressed upon you, and not only wine. Advice of every kind is also offered – whether you ask for it or not – since it is assumed that your education is probably lacking, and that you need a little help in matters that only a Frenchman fully understands.

There is the truffle, for instance, the *Tuber melanosporum*, also known as the 'divine tubercule'. How would I, coming from a country that this delicacy has chosen to avoid, know that the truffle cannot be cultivated? It grows where it pleases, defying all attempts at artificial production. That is why crops and prices vary so much from year to year. My instructor across the table nodded, as though he personally had played a part in the natural order of things.

I asked him what he thought about the genetically modified food that was very much in the news at the time, and he reared back in his chair. It was as if I had insulted his grand-mother or, perhaps worse, his local soccer team. Tampering with nature, he said. No good can come of it. It is nothing but a plot to prevent the process of reproduction, so that farmers have to buy new seeds every year. A *scandale*, promoted by men in white coats, agricultural bandits who never get their hands dirty. He looked set to rant for hours, if he didn't choke on his wine first.

He was silenced by the arrival of an omelette, steaming and fragrant and generously speckled with crunchy black slivers of truffle. It was a vibrant, bright yellow, the yellow that only comes from the yolks of eggs laid by free-range hens, and the consistency had been exquisitely judged by the chef, just on the firm side of runny. The technical term for this is *baveuse* (which sounds much more appetizing than its literal translation – dribbling), and it is a texture that has eluded me for years.

My omelettes, no matter how solicitous I am as I hover over them, are never any more than scrambled eggs with pre-tensions. They don't even travel well, usually falling to pieces during their brief journey to the plate. I have never been able to achieve the plump, moist, soft-skinned golden envelope that slides so cleanly from the pan. I asked my neighbours at the table if they knew the secret. How does one make the perfect omelette?

The ensuing debate lasted for most of lunch, as I should have known it would. There is never a single, simple answer in France to any question concerning food. Ask how to boil an egg, and there will be a dozen different opinions, because there is nothing the French enjoy more than arguing about food while they're at the table. Part of this, I'm convinced, is the opportunity it offers to use the accessories of eating for dramatic gestures. Brandishing a knife is far more satisfying than wagging the conventional index finger; setting down a wineglass (empty, one hopes) with a decisive thump has the emphasis of an exclamation mark; the manoeuvering of pepper pots, mustard jars, saucers of olives, and crusts of bread can often help to demonstrate a complicated theory to the simpleton sitting opposite you. Today's simpleton, of course, was me.

My closest neighbour picked up his side plate and placed one end of his fork on the rim. Holding his creation in one hand, with the fork acting as a makeshift handle, he swirled it around energetically. 'With the omelette,' he said, '*l'essentiel* is the correct pan, which must be made of cast iron.'

'No, no, no,' said the woman sitting next to him. 'Copper, lined with tin, is in every way superior to your cast iron; it's lighter, and a copper bottom is a better conductor of heat. Therefore, *cher monsieur* . . .' she paused to poke a finger in his chest, '. . . your omelette is more evenly cooked. *Voilà.*' She nodded as she looked around the table, obviously feeling she had delivered a mortal blow to any misguided supporters of cast iron.

Already I could see where I might have been going wrong. My omelette pan was made from a new-fangled non-stick aluminium alloy. I'd bought it in America, unable to resist the salesman. 'What you have here is space-age technology,' he had told me. 'If this baby sticks, you come and see me, and I'll give you your money back. Every cent.' Sure enough, it never did stick. But it never made much of an omelette, either. Even so, I decided to try the idea on the experts. 'My pan is a kind of aluminium,' I said. 'What do you think about that?'

Monsieur cast iron and Madame copper bottom forgot their differences and closed ranks, united in their derision. Shakes of the head, clicks of the tongue, smiles of pity. *Non. Jamais.*

Lunch continued, as did the omelette lesson. A new pan must be seasoned two or three times with oil to seal the surface; before putting in the eggs, the pan must be pre-heated until it is hot enough to make a drop of water bounce; the pan must never be washed after use, just wiped with a paper towel. On these basic points, there was general agreement.

Major differences of opinion, marked by knife-waving, glass-banging and head-shaking, started when the lesson moved on to the actual cooking process. Someone insisted that no omelette was complete without a drop of good Madeira wine, stirred in with the eggs before they went into the pan. *Pas du tout*, said a purist, waving his fork – Madeira wasn't necessary; just salt, pepper, and a walnut-sized knob of butter. Ah, but don't forget: the butter should be almost melted before it is allowed to meet with the eggs. Then there is the other knob of butter, which is already in the pan, turning brown. *Mais attention!* It must never smoke, or become too brown, otherwise the omelette will have a burned flavour. And one must always use a wooden spoon to stir the eggs. *Nonsense!* said a woman at the table. A fork is much better when it comes to folding the omelette. *Excusez-moi, madame!* I myself have used a wooden spoon for twenty-five years. *Ah bon?* I've used a fork for thirty years. Game, set and match to Madame, or so I thought.

But no. The fusillade of contradictory opinions continued over three courses – a daube, cheese and dessert. It left me thoroughly confused, despite the thoughtful gift of a set of indecipherable instructions scrawled on the torn-off corner of a paper napkin. When I emerged from the smoky fug of the village hall into the chilly air of late afternoon, the only clear thought in my head was that I'd been using the wrong kind of pan. Space-age technology was no match for a copper bottom.

On the way home, I thought about some of my other religious experiences, starting with daily doses of chapel at school (twice on Sunday, with a thundering sermon thrown in, warning us boys of unspecified but intriguing sins). This had been followed over the years by the usual sporadic mixture of weddings, christenings, and funerals. Most of these had been moving in one way or another, happy or sad, according to the occasion. But I had never before been to a church where there was standing room only, and where there was such a feeling of obvious enjoyment. I couldn't help thinking that the French church attendance record of 10 per cent might well be improved by the promise of a good lunch after the service.

The final word on my visit to Richerenches came from Monsieur Farigoule, when I saw him a few days later. He was obviously curious about my religious habits, and he was determined to know exactly which church I'd been to, and why it had been chosen for what he described as my 'miraculous conversion'.

'Well,' I said, 'it wasn't entirely my choice. It was just the right time to go to this particular church.'

'Aha! So you felt yourself called! By a supernatural force! Remarkable.'

'It certainly was.'

Farigoule looked at me with a slightly puzzled expression. I had the feeling he was thinking that he might, just possibly, have misjudged me. 'Remarkable,' he said again.

I suppose I could have left it at that, and thereby added a much-needed halo to my reputation. But I couldn't keep it up; Farigoule's questions became more and more insistent, and so eventually, reluctantly, I gave in and revealed all.

Perhaps it was a defeat, but Farigoule's gratification made it well worth while. He was thrilled. He inflated visibly, as politicians do in front of television cameras, and, like them, he preened. He had been right all along. Nodding, in the smug and infuriating way of a man who is delighted to have his worst suspicions confirmed, he delivered his closing remarks. 'Of course,' he said. 'Food. I might have known.'

3

Rendezvous in a muddy field

I HAVE A great fondness for *boudin noir*, which I think of as one of the aristocrats of the sausage family – a blood sausage made with pork, usually served on a warm bed of thinly sliced cooked apples. Smooth and rich and dark, it is a dish to be eaten in front of the fire on a day when there is frost on the ground and an icy wind butting against the shutters. Comfort food.

It was winter, and lovers of the blood sausage were coming from every corner of France to take part in the thirty-eighth

Foire au Boudin at Mortagne au Perche, not far from Alencon, the town of lace. The fair was a three-day spree, a kind of extended sausage beauty contest, with breaks for a pig race, a hog-calling competition, a *soirée disco* and several other delights. It sounded wonderful. Unfortunately, the dates clashed with another, much more modest *boudin* festival in the village of Monthureux, north of Dijon – and this was the festival I felt I had to attend, for a single reason.

The great draw, and the highlight of the event, was to be the appearance of the *Grand Mangeur de Boudin* – a human boa constrictor, a one-man sausage demolition squad, a gentleman who, so it was claimed, could eat a metre and a half of *boudin* in fifteen minutes. A metre and a half is a fraction under five feet, and the circumference of a competition-standard *boudin* is approximately the same as that of a fifty-gauge Havana cigar. That's a lot of sausage.

I couldn't believe that any man was capable of dealing with it in a whole day, let alone fifteen minutes. Did he bite, chew, and swallow, or did he just suck it down inch by inch like a giant strand of spaghetti? Whatever his technique, watching him do it would be a memorable sight, one I felt I shouldn't miss. I made travel plans, promising my wife that I'd bring home enough *boudin* to last us until spring.

The *Grand Mangeur* was scheduled to appear at 11.30 on Sunday morning, and to make sure I didn't miss the first bite, I decided to go up to Dijon the night before, which involved an hour's drive to Avignon station and then two hours on the train. When I arrived, I rented a car. Judging by the map, Monthureux looked to be about two hours from Dijon, so I'd have plenty of time to get there in the morning. I even found a restaurant not far from the hotel that had *boudin* on the menu. Everything was under control. For once, the assignment was proceeding like clockwork.

The next morning was foul: grey skies and driving sleet, nobody on the streets of Dijon, very few cars on the road. It was a truly miserable start to the day. Never mind, I told myself. This is ideal weather for lunch, and there will undoubtedly be some kindred spirits in Monthureux, a glass or two of wine, and more *boudin* than most people see in a lifetime. I drove on. The sky grew darker, the sleet more intense, the countryside emptier.

I stopped in a small town for coffee, and to buy a local paper, expecting to find some reference to the *boudin* festival: an advertisement, perhaps, or a pre-bout interview with the *Grand Mangeur*. But curiously, there was no mention of historic events in the *boudin* world. I returned to the car, set the windscreen wipers on overdrive, and pressed on through the sleet.

It was just before 11.00 when I reached Monthureux. I had planned to spend half an hour or so getting the feel of the place and talking to other *boudin* fanciers before the excitement started, but it was curiously quiet for a village *en fête*. Actually, it was quieter than quiet. It was completely deserted. The mayor must have been overwhelmed by the number of people who were coming to the fair, and had therefore decided to hold the celebrations in a hall outside the village, somewhere large enough to accommodate a crowd. That would explain why I hadn't seen a single soul on the streets. I drove on.

Nobody. Nothing. No banners, no posters of smiling pigs, no hint of jolly activity. Just one wet, empty field after another. I drove back through the village and out the other side before I saw a sign of human life, at a distance, a moving bump on the sodden horizon.

It was a man driving a tractor. Surely he would know where the action was. Up and down the field he went, gradually getting closer. I waited at the edge of a sea of freshly ploughed mud, waving at him beneath my umbrella. He stopped the tractor when he was fifty yards away and sat in the shelter of the driver's cabin, staring. He clearly wasn't going to get out. I tiptoed through the mud until I was close enough to speak to him.

'I wonder if you can help me. I'm looking for the *Foire au Boudin*.'

He leaned forward in his seat to study the dripping apparition looking up at him. '*Comment?*'

'You know, the sausage fair. The one with the *Grand Mangeur*.'

He pushed his cap back, leaving a smear of mud on his forehead. The corners of his mouth went down, his shoulders came up – every Frenchman's way of telling you he doesn't know and doesn't particularly care.

I felt the beginnings of panic. 'This *is* Monthureux, isn't it?'

He nodded. 'One of them.'

'There are more?'

'This is Monthureux-sur-Saône. There is also Monthureux-le-Sec.' He jerked a thumb over his shoulder. 'It's a long way, over near Vittel. For all I know, there may be others.' He nodded again, adjusted his cap, put the tractor into gear, and chugged off to resume his communion with the horizon.

By now, the *Grand Mangeur*, wherever he might be, would be loosening up with a few chipolatas before moving on to the main challenge. I stood, moist and muddy, watching the tractor disappear into the murk. I had blown it. The expedition had been a disaster, but I was too wet to worry about it. They say that missed pleasures only heighten the anticipation of pleasures to come, but all I wanted was to get back to Dijon and into a dry pair of socks.

4

The thigh-tasters of Vittel

CONSIDER THE FROG; neither fish nor fowl but something in between, a symbol to many people of gastronomic eccentricity, and a creature that is still used by the British to identify an entire nation. 'The Frogs', we call the French, often with a quiver of horror at their curious appetites. 'They'll eat anything.'

Living in the southern part of France, where there is more sun than water, it is rare to meet a frog on a menu. He thrives in the damp, mates in his pond, spends his moist life in a temperate climate. The chances of finding him in a Provençal kitchen are remote. So when I decided to test the truth of the old chestnut – 'actually, it tastes like chicken' – I had to go north, a long way north.

The plumpest and most desirable frogs in France, so I was

told, live in the Vosges. Here in the north-east of the country is a curvaceous, green region that nature has supplied with mountains, rivers, and thousands of *étangs* – mere patches of water to us, but extremely well suited to the residential requirements of the frog. This, in turn, has made the area a magnet, once a year, for frog-fanciers. They come to the Vosges from all over Europe on the last Sunday in April, gathering in the town of Vittel to celebrate their passion.

Vittel is best known for its therapeutic calcium-rich water. It is normally associated with *la cure* – two weeks or so of undemanding walks or bicycle rides in the park, with perhaps an excursion to the casino for a little light gambling. These activities are accompanied, needless to say, by the steady consumption of bottle after bottle of the local tonic, bathing the liver, flushing the pipes, bringing a healthy bloom to the complexion. Not surprisingly, the personality of the town is usually calm. Visitors are recovering from their digestive sins, and they move slowly, even on yellow rented bicycles. The two public toilets on the main street do a brisk business as the water does its work, but there is no other evidence of anyone in a hurry. Peace reigns.

This was about to change on the day I arrived in Vittel. It was grey and cool and overcast; fine weather for frogs, according to an amateur meteorologist nursing a beer in one of the cafés. In the side streets, workmen were setting up the mobile paraphernalia that every self-respecting *fête* requires: the shooting galleries and merry-go-rounds, the stands selling souvenirs and snacks, the long tents with trestle tables for more elaborate eating – which in this case would be frogs.

Many frogs. If previous years were anything to go by, nearly thirty thousand people would get through five tons of frogs by the end of the fair.

An entire double-page spread in the local newspaper was dominated by frogs in their various manifestations. One, dressed in a demure striped swimsuit of Victorian cut, promised dream clothes at the Mod'In boutique. An advertisement for the Vittel gym featured a muscular frog lifting weights, and it promised *belles cuisses* to anyone following his example. Beautiful thighs, as I was to discover, were highly prized and would often be referred to, with many a wink and a waggle of the eyebrows, over the next couple of days. Another advertisement listed eight different ways in which these delicacies could be enjoyed – poached in Riesling, in quiches, under a crisp gratin with asparagus, with noodles and snails, even *à la provençale*, a thigh for every imaginable taste. On the same page, superimposed over the figure of a smiling and nubile frog in the classic position of the reclining nude, was the announcement that Miss Grenouille (or, as some admirers would call her, Miss Cuisse) would be elected shortly after the official Sunday lunch. And there was to be a *grenouillade monstre* that very evening in the Salle du Moulin, under the auspices of the brotherhood of thigh-tasters. In every sense of the word, it looked like it would be a full weekend.

I had made an appointment with the president and thigh-taster-in-chief, Monsieur Loisant, and found him supervising preparations in the Salle du Moulin. A slim, lively man, he seemed pleased to have another nationality to add to his list of foreign visitors. There were Belgians, Dutch, Germans, even Portuguese, but I was his first and only Englishman. And the word had spread. As I was on my way to meet him, I passed two workmen setting up tables in one of the tents. 'They say there's an Englishman here this year,' one of them said. 'Ah *bon*,' said the other, in a tone of utter disinterest. 'I'll tell the frogs.'

In between trips to the kitchen at the back of the hall, where thighs by the trayful were being stacked alongside the ovens, Loisant told me how Vittel had become a Mecca for frog-lovers.

'It started twenty-seven years ago,' he said. 'René Clement, who ran the restaurant just down the road, had a little *étang* on his land. One spring day back in 1972, he found his *étang* invaded. Hundreds of frogs! More than he had ever seen! What was he to do?'

'Well,' I said, 'as he was a chef . . .'

'Exactly! He set up a table on the terrace outside his restaurant. He cooked – *mon Dieu*, how he cooked – nothing but frogs' legs and maybe some *pommes frites*. He fed *le tout* Vittel. Next year, the same. So it went on. Now, as you know, we have our own *confrérie* with two hundred and fifty members.' He looked at his watch, then turned to go back to the kitchen. 'Meet me tomorrow morning, nine o'clock at the Palais des Congrès. There will be breakfast with a little white wine, and then the parade. You will be our first English *confrère*.'

I wasn't at all sure that this distinction was deserved. I could hardly claim to be a connoisseur, or even a regular consumer, and to be elevated at a single hop into the aristocracy

of frog-eaters was an unexpected honour. It was also something of a change in status. Normally, my role in these affairs
is simply that of an observer, unknown and, ideally, unnoticed, a bystander scribbling furtive notes. But this time, I
was to be in the thick of things, nibbling thighs in front of an
audience. And what else would I be required to do? Loisant
had given me no particular instructions apart from telling me
to turn up for breakfast the following morning. But I had
been a spectator at one or two ceremonies in which friends
had been elected as *confrères*, and I knew that initiation ritu-
als were often rich in potentially humiliating moments:
draining a monstrous goblet of red wine without dribbling or
pausing for breath, reciting from memory an oath of alle-
giance in Provençal, singing the anthem of the *confrérie* – all
these I had seen from the comfortable anonymity of the
watching crowd. And now the crowd would be watching me.

While it was impossible to imagine exactly what form the
initiation ceremony would take, one part of it was entirely
predictable. Without a doubt, I would be called upon to eat –
not only to eat, but to eat with conspicuous relish – at least a
couple of thighs, maybe more. I could remember coming up
against frogs' legs only once before, and an overpowering
experience it had been too, rather like sucking garlic-flavoured
lollipops. But that was the work of an amateur cook, unused to
the finer points of *cuisine grenouille*. Here in frog heartland, the
local chefs would doubtless have a more delicate touch.
Encouraged by the thought, I decided to have a trial run, to get
in some private practice before my public debut.

Although the restaurants of Vittel that evening were united

in their homage to the frog, I found myself drawn instead to one of the stands in a side street. Canvas had been stretched over a scaffolding framework, with long plank tables arranged in front of a makeshift counter. Most of the seats were already taken, and I noticed that the style of the evening was to wear one's paper napkin tucked into the shirt collar, which in France is usually the sign of a man who takes his food seriously. There was just the right mixture of music and laughter. Bonhomie was in the air, bottles of Riesling on the tables, frogs' legs on the menu. I took an empty seat next to a group of large and boisterous men – members of a rugby club, according to their T-shirts – and gave my order to the waitress.

My accent caused my neighbour to turn towards me, his head cocked. He had the slightly ravaged ears of a front row forward who had been in the middle of too many rugby scrums, and a broad, good-natured face.

'Where are you from?' he asked.

'I'm English.' This with a certain amount of apprehension, as rugby matches between France and England tend to be replays of the battle of Agincourt, and passions of both players and supporters run high. Fortunately, my neighbour didn't seem to bear any grudges.

'Ah, *les anglais*,' he said. '*Ils sont durs*. They play like tanks.' I think it was meant as a compliment, because he filled my glass from the bottle in front of him. 'And what are you doing here?'

When I told him I was anxious to learn about frogs, he let out a rumble of laughter and nudged his friend. An

Englishman who was interested in frogs. What could be more bizarre?

As I've often said, there is nothing a Frenchman likes more than a self-confessed ignoramus, preferably foreign, who can be instructed in the many marvels and curiosities of France. I think it must be part of the national psyche, a compulsion to educate and thus to civilize those who have suffered the misfortune of being born in a less privileged part of the world. It happens all the time in Provence, where I have received free tuition in subjects as varied as the skinning of red peppers, the extinction of rats, the treatment of ailing plane trees, the training of truffle hounds and the correct way to administer a suppository (*doucement, doucement*). Now it was about to happen again.

After a moment or two of muttering to his friend and another grunt of laughter, my neighbour turned back to me. The first thing to know, he said, is never to leave frogs in your hotel bedroom. *Jamais.*

I nodded. It was undoubtedly a very bad habit to get into. And then he told me why.

Some friends of his had been away from home on a job near Lyon, draining a large reservoir before starting work on the restoration of an old chateau. It was spring, and the reservoir was teeming with frogs – succulent young creatures, an opportunity too tasty to pass up. One of the men, wise in the ways of the frog, knew exactly what to do. A length of red cloth was purchased, then torn into small pieces. These were tied to the ends of bamboo rods, and issued to each man, together with instructions on technique.

It was not unlike fly fishing, a gentle cast that left the scraps of cloth bobbing on the surface of the reservoir. And the frogs bit. Whether they were attracted by the colour or by the cloth or by the method of dragging it slowly across the water wasn't made clear to me, but, one after another, the frogs rose to the bait. By the time evening fell, several large plastic bags had been filled.

The idea was to take them home the following day, to be cooked and eaten over the weekend. But that night, the workmen were staying the night in a small hotel close to the building site. It was a Friday, and the men went out to celebrate the end of a hard week, leaving the frogs to amuse themselves in one of the hotel rooms.

And amuse themselves they did. Leaping from the restrictive confines of the plastic bags, they enjoyed the freedom of the room. Signs of their passage were discovered later; on pillows and bedspreads and night tables, over the top of the television set, across the phone, everywhere. And then, no doubt made peckish by their explorations, they had looked for something to eat. Passing up the sheets and pillowcases, and not tempted by the carpet, they chose instead to gorge on the wallpaper – a faded print made tender by the passage of years enlivened, no doubt, by a soupçon of mature, crispy glue.

Returning after dinner, the workman whose room it was found the lower parts of the walls stripped clean. Replete and sleepy frogs covered the floor, blinking at the light and far from pleased at being disturbed. Collecting them to put back in their bags took up a good part of the night. The workmen left early the following morning, leaving the hotel management to puzzle over the adjustments that had been made to the décor.

It wasn't the best story to hear just before starting a dinner of frogs' legs, and I looked with a certain amount of suspicion at the plate that had been put in front of me. The legs, which had been sautéed in white wine, were cream-coloured and flecked with parsley. They looked appetizing and smelled delicious, but I couldn't help wondering what kind of diet had made them so firm and well rounded. Was wallpaper the secret ingredient? Old phone bills? Or had they been fattened up on sheet after sheet of virginal, top-quality Kleenex?

'*Allez,*' said my neighbour. 'With the fingers.'

In fact, as the tiny legs had been served on the bone, using a knife and fork would have required the skills of a micro-surgeon. So I did as I was told, picking up a leg and taking my first tentative bite.

Chicken? Not exactly. It seemed to have a finer texture than chicken, and tasted smoother. It was moist, it was tender, and it was flavoured with a well-judged tingle of garlic – altogether different from those explosively seasoned thighs I remembered eating years before.

I finished the first leg and put it down, conscious that my neighbour was watching closely.

'No, no,' he said. 'Suck the bone.' He lifted one hand to his lips and bunched his fingertips into a bouquet. 'It's good.'

Walking back through the streets of Vittel after dinner, there was no escaping the frog. There he was, crouching in the windows of *patisseries*, fashioned from marzipan or chocolate;

starring in all the menus that were displayed outside restaurants; bright green and inappropriately furry, as a prize in the
shooting galleries. I stopped by *the grenouillade monstre* in the
Salle du Moulin, and there he was again, three feet high, wearing a top hat and clutching a bottle, beaming across the room
above a low-lying fog bank of cigarette smoke. I wouldn't have
been surprised to encounter him, jaunty and relieved, in the
toilettes publiques. But the tiled walls were bare of any humor-
ous posters, possibly because evacuation, being part of the
cure, is not a joking matter in Vittel.

There was a uniformed presence in town that night – not,
as one might have expected, patrolling gendarmes to make
sure the revelry didn't get out of hand, but a squad of Pastis
51 salesmen. Distinguished by their red jackets and their
cheerful diligence with the bottle, they were offering *dégustations*: a free nip to anyone feeling the need of a change from
beer or Reisling. One over-refreshed gentleman, the benefici-
ary of several nips, stood in the doorway of a bar calling
loudly for an accordion so that he could entertain passers-by.
The owner of the bar countered by turning up the volume of
his jukebox. Affronted, the would-be accordionist glared at
the source of the noise, lit the wrong end of a filter-tipped cigarette, and lurched off in search of artistic fulfilment
elsewhere.

Sometime after midnight, the crowds had thinned, and I
went back to the hotel. Leaning out of my window, I heard
the distant fairground music give a wheeze and an electronic
grunt before coming to a stop. The night sky was encouraging, clear enough to give some hope for good weather the

following day, with the light from a solitary star coming and going through wisps of cloud like blinks of celestial neon.

Vittel and its visitors were in luck. The morning started bright and sunny, and it was almost hot by the time I reached the Palais des Congrès just before nine. While I was waiting in line to register, I was handed a list of the *confréries* that were putting in an official appearance to give fraternal support. There were fifty-seven of them altogether, most of them from various parts of France, some with highly impressive titles, like the Chevaliers du Brie and the Companions of the Black Sausage. The rest of Europe was represented by *confrères* from Portugal, Switzerland, Belgium and Holland – but, as I had already discovered, nobody from Britain but myself.

The idea of a convivial association based on the enjoyment of gastronomic specialties seems to hold no great appeal for the British, and I wondered why not. It may be true that we don't produce as many edible treasures as the French, but we have our moments. Why aren't they officially marked? Where are the Companions of the Fish and Chip? The Honourable Brotherhood of Yorkshire Pudding? The Noble Order of Cheddar? The Commanders of the Winkle and the Whelk? The Friends of the Jellied Eel?

'*Bonjour*,' said a voice from below me, 'you're the Englishman.'

I looked down to find that I'd reached the head of the line and the check-in desk. A smartly dressed man smiled up at me, introduced himself as Jean Pierre Roussel, and told me that I couldn't have a drink until I'd answered a few questions about my background and signed on as a future *confrère*. With these formalities over, he nodded me over to the bar.

Alcohol with breakfast is dangerously pleasant. My first experience of it had been some years before as a guest of the mayor of Bouzy, a village in the Champagne region. There had been two different wines to accompany the food, and politeness obliged me to sample them both. They were cool and invigorating, slipping down easily despite the earliness of the hour, and I was in a happy haze by 9.00 a.m. Lunch – and more wine, naturally – had been served just in time to prevent a return to sobriety, and I ended the day in disgrace after falling asleep at dinner. Since then, I've done my best to stick to coffee in the mornings.

The area in front of the bar was crowded with men and women I took to be *confrères*. At this stage, they were still wearing civilian clothes, except for a blond Labrador, very chic and apparently quite comfortable in a well-cut waistcoat of royal blue satin, that was standing guard below a dish of croissants in case one should fall from the table. According to his owner, the Labrador was an old hand at these events. The waistcoat was part of the regalia of another distinguished order, and this was to be his third time as a *confrère*. I asked if he liked frogs' legs.

'Monsieur,' said his owner, 'he is a Labrador. He likes everything.'

By now, there were signs of preparation among my future colleagues, who were starting to line up before taking their turn in the cloakrooms. Men and women of conservative

appearance went in. Peacocks came out.

The frog contingent wore caps and cloaks of a bright and froggy green, edged with yellow, but this was one of the more sober outfits. I saw cloaks trimmed with silver and something that looked very much like ermine, cloaks of silk, and cloaks of velvet. Official decorations were worn, massive medals that clanked against one another as they bounced up and down on the wearer's sternum. And hats. My God, what hats – troubadours' floppy berets, tricornes, fedoras of medieval design which were pierced with great swooping feathers, straw bonnets, and one creation of truly outstanding frivolity, more of a giggle than a hat. It consisted of what looked like two small pillows made from pink plush that hung from a purple headband so that they covered the ears and rested on the shoulders of the wearer (a gentleman who was probably a highly respectable judge or tax inspector in real life). The hat was worn with a purple cloak, baggy Elizabethan-style bloomers, and tights. It will give you some idea of the mood of the morning, as well as the variety of sartorial treasures on display, when I tell you that this extraordinary apparition attracted no particular attention.

With a final swig of Riesling and one last adjustment to the tilt of a hat or the drape of a cloak, the assembled *confrères* moved outside to form lines of three abreast for the opening event of the proceedings. This was a parade that would take us through Vittel for a rendezvous with the mayor. He had invited us all to join him for a drink at the *mairie*, an alcoholic bridge between the wine at breakfast and the wine at lunch.

But first there was the length of the town to negotiate in correct ceremonial order. The procession was led by a small but impressively loud marching band, their brass instruments gleaming against the red and black of their uniforms. They were followed by Les Majorettes de Vittel, encouraged in their twirlings and baton-tossing by a watchful coach, from the look of her an ex-twirler herself, who hovered alongside hissing technical advice. '*Haut les genoux!*' Lift those knees!

And then came the *confrères*. Foreigners had been given precedence, and I found myself at the front of the procession among a group of Portuguese, Belgians and Dutch. We congratulated one another on the sunshine, a contrast to some parades of the past when rain had caused headgear to wilt and dispositions to droop. Today was perfect, bright and breezy, with the sound of the band and the sight of the majorettes to sustain us on our way.

For the first few hundred yards all went well, and a brave sight it must have been, feathers and cloaks fluttering, medals twinkling, and the uniformed Labrador – now wearing a cap to match his waistcoat – receiving much encouragement from the crowd. We were managing to maintain a disciplined marching order that would have done credit to Napoleon's troops, when suddenly there was a *crise de baton*. One of the majorettes attempted an over-ambitious toss, and the baton went astray, ending up among the spectators. The majorettes came to a sudden stop. Ahead of them, the band marched on, unaware of the enforced halt. Behind them, the procession of *confrères* contracted like a human concertina. We waited while the baton was retrieved, a pause just long enough for my neighbouring *confrère* to unscrew his ceremonial staff and hand me the hollow top. 'Do you like *pastis*?' he asked, tipping up the staff and filling the top. 'I make it myself.' The top was passed around, emptied, and screwed back on while the majorettes resumed formation, and off we went again, on the double this time to catch up with the distant band.

The end of the march was marked by a ribbon stretched across the street, with Monsieur le Maire waiting on the other side, smile and scissors at the ready. The band played a suitably triumphant piece, cameras clicked, and the ribbon was cut. It was time to move on to the next and perhaps most important part of the programme: the initiation of new thigh-tasters.

The town hall was fragrant with the scent of freshly cooked frogs' legs, and I saw my fellow-*confrère* the Labrador stop for a long and thoughtful sniff as he came through the door. He seemed completely at ease in his cap and waistcoat, wagging politely to his neighbours as he took his place in the front row, reserved for VIPs.

Up on the stage, Monsieur Roussel, the master of ceremonies, made final adjustments to the microphone while senior members of the order lined up behind him next to the president, Monsieur Loisant. Expressions were serious, befitting the solemnity of the moment, and the spectators did their best to assume an expectant hush as Roussel opened the proceedings.

Solemnity didn't last long. The ritual of initiation starts with some brief and not always flattering comments about each of the new *confrères*, the more embarrassing the better, and Roussel had done his homework. One after the other, he called his victims up on stage to describe their backgrounds and achievements, their follies and idiosyncracies, even their physical appearance (with a special emphasis on the state of their thighs). The *confrère* was then asked to eat a small dish of frogs' legs, drink a glass of Chardonnay and swear fidelity to the frog before receiving his medal and retiring to welcome obscurity at the back of the stage.

An hour or so passed, until the only remaining new *confrères* were myself and the Labrador. He behaved with the aplomb you would expect from a dog that had already been honoured twice before – scampering up on the stage and polishing off his frogs' legs in two great gulps – his performance only slightly marred by turning up his nose at the Chardonnay. And then it was my turn. I made my way on to the stage, feeling very dowdy among the robes and velvet caps in my jacket and flannels. Even the Labrador was better dressed for the occasion than I was.

Roussel dealt with me gently, possibly because he hadn't had the chance to discover anything truly incriminating about me. In any case, my nationality was enough to give him plenty of material, since the French and the English have

enjoyed saying appalling things about each other for several
hundred years. Curiously enough, they're often the same
appalling things. For instance, each accuses the other of arrogance, bloody-mindedness, unashamed chauvinism, and
barbaric eating habits. The French say the English are cold-
blooded and untrustworthy. The English say the French are
hot-headed and untrustworthy. But, as Roussel said, close
neighbours are often a little hard on each other, and he let me
off with no more than a passing rap across the knuckles for
having ignored one of the great delicacies of France – the
frog – for most of my adult life.

I ate my thighs, I drank my Chardonnay, and then I bowed
my head to receive my medal. I had become an official
member of the *Confrérie des Taste Cuisses de Grenouilles de
Vittel*, the first organization I had belonged to since the age of
eleven, when I left the Boy Scouts under a cloud after a personality clash with Leaping Wolf.

And now, as if the various tipples of the morning hadn't
been enough, the moment had arrived to have a drink with
the mayor. This time, no attempt was made to form an orderly
line. The spectators, who hadn't been dosed with Chardonnay
up on stage and were pawing the ground for something wet to
settle the dust of all those speeches, led the charge over to the
mairie. His Honour, supported by the Pastis 51 lobby in their
red coats, received us with open bottles and yet another
speech, while *confrères* loosened their cloaks and flexed their
medals. The cheerful atmosphere provided no hint of the
drama that was about to unfold on the very steps of the
mairie.

In fact, it was some time before those of us who had drifted back to the Palais des Congrès, where lunch was to be served, had any idea that a drama had actually taken place. But as we found our seats and deliberated over the choice of aperitif, it became clear that all was not well. Whispered conversations were taking place in corners, with much glancing at watches.

Waitresses had to be restrained from descending on us with the first course. Looking around the room I saw that every seat was taken – except one. Loisant, thigh-taster-in-chief and our esteemed president, was missing.

What could have happened to him on the five-minute stroll from the *mairie*? Rumour and theory spread from table to table with the speed of a brush fire, but nothing prepared us for his eventual appearance. He came through the door looking like a man who'd just lost an argument with a hammer, his forehead bruised and swollen, his right eye puffy and half-closed, black stitches visible against discoloured skin.

The presidential sense of humour, however, was uninjured, and as he took his place at the head of the table he explained that he had been wounded in the course of duty. Coming out of the *mairie*, he had been ambushed by a snail – *un perfide escargot* – which was lying in wait on one of the steps. He remembered hearing two crunches: one as his foot crushed and then skidded on the snail's shell, the other as his head cracked against the stone. But after a trip to the hospital for repair work, he claimed to be as good as new and hungry as a lion.

'I have heard,' said the lady sitting on my left, 'that although the frog is not popular in your country, the English have a fondness for eating toads.' She shuddered. 'How could you possibly eat a toad?'

This put a stop to all other conversation at our end of the table. Heads turned towards me as I tried to describe the only toad recipe I'd ever heard of – *crapaud dans le trou*, or toad in the hole, a leaden dish that I had been made to eat once or twice in my youth. As I remembered the recipe, a large ball of sausage meat is concealed inside a thick coating of rubbery batter before being thoroughly overcooked. The result is not unlike a booby-trapped Yorkshire pudding; heavy, stodgy, and highly indigestible.

'Ah,' said the lady, 'so it is not a veritable toad.'

'No,' I said. A veritable toad would probably have tasted better.

'Nor is it, strictly speaking, a hole.'

'I'm afraid not,' I said.

She shook her head at the peculiarities of traditional English cuisine and we went back to studying the menu. In honour of the occasion, this offered not only the list of dishes – including, of course, sautéed frogs' legs – but some artistic nourishment as well, in the form of a poem specially composed by Roussel – *Odes à Mesdames les Grenouilles*. Written with tongue firmly in cheek, it was couched in the language of romance: '*Tendre grenouille de nos étangs,*' it began, and then flowed into the springtime song of love and the arrival of Prince Charming before the inevitable occurred and our heroine was summoned to meet her fate in the kitchen. Even here, she was not just cooked but also transformed by the poet into 'the queen of our plates', which I hope was some small consolation to her.

The unfortunate Prince Charming also came to a sticky end, according to one version of frog legend. Once upon a time, so the story goes, a beautiful princess came across a frog by the side of a pond. Said the frog to the princess, 'I was once a handsome young prince, until an evil witch put a spell on me. But one kiss from you, and I will turn back into a prince. Then we can marry and move into the castle with my mother. You can prepare my meals, scrub my clothes, clean up after me, bear my children, cook for my friends and live happily ever after. Just one kiss, and all this will come to pass.' That night at dinner, the princess smiled to herself. Not bloody likely, she thought, as she tucked in to a dish of frogs' legs.

Wine and conversation flowed, the courses came and went, and I was treated to a demonstration of the French genius for the gastronomic marathon, the ability to spend as long at the table as other nationalities spend watching television. The size of French appetites never fails to impress me, nor does the Frenchman's ability to absorb vast amounts of alcohol without falling head first into the cheese. The physical effects of a river of wine are evident in flushed complexions and loosened collars, in louder voices and more risqué jokes, but I've never seen any ugly or argumentative behaviour. Perhaps the secret is years of practice.

By now, the accordion band was starting to limber up with a few exploratory riffs, and I saw that Loisant and his master of ceremonies, the poetic Roussel, had left their table to take up positions at the edge of the dance floor. Chairs were pushed back, glasses were refilled, and the microphone was switched on. It was the moment of truth in the contest to see who had the most delectable thighs in Vittel.

The judging criteria, so I had been told, were more or less the same for Miss Grenouille as for a frog. Any thigh with half a chance had to be long, but not skinny, and shapely, but not fat. Tone and texture were of crucial importance, and the judges were not to be influenced by any fashionable embell-ishments such as tattoos. A smooth, unmarked sweep of thigh was what they were looking for, and it was clear from the president's confident manner that this exemplary specimen had been found.

'*Mesdames, Messieurs!*' Roussel had our attention, and I half expected him to burst into verse, despite the difficulties of finding words to rhyme with *cuisses*. Instead, he confined himself to a brief introduction that ended with a stirring drumroll as Miss Grenouille herself was announced, and came tripping across the floor to receive an enormous bou-quet from the hands of the president. Amelie was her name, and a delightful young lady she was too, smiling and rosy-cheeked from the applause. Alas, the prize-winning thighs were encased in tight black toreador pants, and therefore more hinted at than revealed. I think there might have been a murmur or two of disappointment from some of the gentlemen connoisseurs in the audience.

But all thoughts of frogs and thighs were now put aside. There was dancing to be done, and the French take their dancing seriously – above all, the *paso doble*. This stately manoeuvre, somewhere between a fox-trot and a tango, is a particular favourite, possibly because it accommodates the Gallic fondness for expressive use of the upper body. Three or four gliding steps are taken in one direction, and then – with a twist of the shoulders, the hint of a shrug and sometimes the flick of a heel – the dancers change course. Movements are smooth and unhurried; correct form is everything. Heads are held up, backs are kept ruler-straight, and elbows are cocked out at right angles. And I noticed that several of the older men had preserved the tradition of extending the little finger of the left hand as they steered their partners in courtly zigzags across the floor. It was a fine sight, and could only have been finer if the dancers had still been dressed in their cloaks and feathered hats.

In this way, Sunday afternoon passed into Sunday evening, and lunch threatened to spill over into dinner. The frog had been well and truly celebrated.

By the following morning, there was little trace of the great *weekend des grenouilles*. The fairground rides and shooting galleries were gone – dismantled, packed up and shipped out overnight. The flow of free *pastis* had dried up with the departure of the gentlemen in red jackets. Restaurants were revising their menus to make them less frog-heavy. Miss Grenouille was back at her job, the president's wound was mending nicely, the *confrères* were on their way home, and the yellow bicycles were being pedalled sedately along the paths of the park. Peace had returned to Vittel.

5
Slow food

AN ADULT SNAIL in prime condition has a top speed of just
over four yards per hour. He is a gastropod, making
his stately progress through life on a single muscular, self-
lubricating foot. He has two sets of horns; the upper set
equipped with eyes, the lower with a sense of smell. He (or just
as often she) is also a hermaphrodite, having the remarkable
and doubtless useful ability to change sex as the occasion
demands. The snail is a curious but harmless creature; its great
misfortune, in France at least, is to be considered a delicacy.

I found these basic facts in a book, an elderly copy of
L'Escargot Comestible. It is a slim, no-nonsense volume
brought out by *La Maison Rustique*, whose other titles include
such gems as *How to Tan the Skins of Small Animals*, *Practical
Salmon Raising*, and *The Capture and Destruction of Moles*. I

think it would be fair to describe the people at *La Maison Rustique* as fringe publishers.

My wife had found the book on a bric-a-brac stand at one of the local markets. Knowing my fascination for the snail, she bought it for me, and I spent an afternoon going through its musty, damp-stained pages. The illustrations were sparse – a couple of anatomical drawings and some faded black-and-white photographs of the snail in two classic poses: hidden inside the shell, or protruding from it. The text was scholarly in tone, and there were no unnecessary typographical flourishes. In other words, it was a serious piece of work, designed to inform students and breeders of the mollusc rather than entertain snail dilettantes like me.

But, serious work though it was, a Frenchman had written it. And so, inevitably, there was a recipe section: *escargots à la sauce bourguignon, à la sauce poulette, à la provençale, à l'espagnole, farcis* – all set out in the same dry, precise, professorial style that had been used to describe the snail's mating habits, sleep patterns and robust digestive system.

It happened that the book arrived at the perfect moment, just after I had received an invitation to the twenty-eighth annual *Foire aux Escargots* at Martigny-les-Bains. The fair is now sufficiently well established to have its own official stationery, and my invitation was decorated with a life-size pair of snails – looking, I thought, rather uncomfortable. The illustrator had dressed them for the occasion in collars and ties, and they had that faintly embarrassed expression one sees on dogs that have been obliged by their owners to wear little tartan raincoats.

As for the programme of events, many diversions were promised at Martigny – edible, musical, and commercial, as well as the beauty contest that is an essential part of these celebrations. Here, the organizers had clearly run up against the problem of what title to give the winner. At the frog fair I went to in Vittel, the prettiest girl was elected Miss Grenouille, which was somehow quite flattering, as frogs are renowned for their long legs and delectable thighs. But Miss Snail? What does that bring to mind? Two pairs of horns, a single muscular foot, and a gelatinous undercarriage – hardly the stuff of which beauty queens are made. Well then, how about Miss Mollusc? No, perhaps not. And Miss Hermaphrodite was absolutely out of the question. The day was eventually saved by choosing to give the winner the title of Miss Coquille. Translated into the prosaic English word 'shell', it might be said to lack glamour, but the French word has a certain saucy sound about it. And besides, even if you can't eat the shell, it is probably the snail's single most attractive feature. So Miss Coquille it was.

Martigny-les-Bains is almost as far northeast as you can go without leaving France. As the names of the villages suggest, it's a watery region. References to baths and springs are everywhere, from Puits-des-Fées (the fairies' well) to Plombières-les-Bains, Grandrupt-de-Bains, and – the ultimate liquid village – Bains-les-Bains.

The complexion of the landscape on that sunny day in May was a testament to the cosmetic benefits of abundant water. It had been a particularly dry and dusty spell in Provence, with two days of rain in three months, and I found the lushness of the northern countryside almost shocking. I must have driven past a hundred shades of green, dark rows of conifers in the distance contrasting with the glowing, luminous bursts of new growth that follow a wet spring. Cream-coloured cows were sunbathing in the fields, lying down so that only their heads were visible above the rich green waves of grass. The ditches on either side of the road overflowed with green. I stopped to check the map. Even most of that was coloured green.

I reached Martigny in the late afternoon. It was hot and quiet, with no obvious indication of the celebrations to come. No posters, no bunting, no strings of coloured lights. For a moment, I wondered if I had come to the right Martigny – there are eight or nine to choose from in France – and then I saw what appeared to be a road sign. It was large and triangular and extremely official-looking. But instead of a warning to motorists, the red border framed two snails with their horns cocked, displaying an air of jaunty well-being. As far as one can judge with snails, they looked as though they hadn't a care in the world.

The French are not normally sentimental about their food, but they do like whatever it is they are about to eat to look happy. (It is, as these fortunate creatures should realize, a great compliment that a Frenchman would consider them worthy of consumption.) Thus, in butchers' shops and market stands, on posters and wrapping paper, you will see anthropomorphic expressions applied to the most unlikely faces. Chickens smile, cows laugh, pigs beam, rabbits wink, and fish smirk. All of them seem to be thrilled that they will be making an important contribution to dinner.

The sign of the snails led me into the main street of Martigny, and I felt the current of curiosity that I'm sure all strangers feel as they walk for the first time through a small French village. Lace curtains flicker in windows, revealing a bright and inquisitive eye that follows you up the street. Conversations stop. Heads turn to inspect someone so obviously from somewhere else. There's nothing unfriendly about it, but you can't help feeling like a sore thumb.

I was looking for Madame Gerard, one of the organizers of the fair, who had given me the Rue des Vosges as a meeting point. Seeing three ladies of the village who were taking a break from gossip to stare at me, I asked them for directions.

'I'm looking for the Rue des Vosges.'

One of the ladies looked at me over the top of her glasses. 'You're standing in it, monsieur.'

'Ah. Then perhaps you could tell me where I could find Madame Gerard?'

One shrug. Two shrugs. Three shrugs. And then, as a car came down the empty street: '*Voilà! Elle arrive.*'

But Madame Gerard was preoccupied. There were problems. These affairs are not without their complications, and she couldn't stop to talk. Later, maybe we could meet at the Hôtel International. And off she went, leaving me with the three ladies. Naturally, they were fascinated. What was a stranger – even more bizarre, a foreign stranger – doing here? Was I as lost as I appeared to be? Was I part of tomorrow's festivities?

I told them I had come to admire the snails, and I was sorry to hear that there were problems. An intake of breath and a shaking of the head from one of the ladies. Let us hope, she said, that they are not as grave as the catastrophe of a few years ago, when the truck bringing snails to Martigny met with an accident and overturned. Two thousand dozen snails! Scattered all over the road! It was *très dramatique*, and only superhuman efforts by the village butcher to arrange a supply of reinforcements saved the fair from disaster. Imagine a snail fair without snails! The thought of it reduced the ladies to silence.

It is possible to walk from one end of Martigny to the other and back again in ten minutes, which I did, keeping an eye open for the Hôtel International, and wondering how a hotel could survive in these quiet green depths of the French countryside. Perhaps it had a clientele of snail fanciers; possibly perhaps a steady trickle of *heliculteurs*, or snail breeders, coming from all over the world to brush up on the latest reproduction techniques. To my disappointment, I saw nothing resembling a hotel, let alone one with such a grand name. But leaning against a van with their arms crossed were two men who had watched me pass by and who were still watching when I came back. They would know where I could find the Hôtel International. I asked them, and for the second time that afternoon felt like a complete bumpkin.

'You're standing in front of it, monsieur.' They jerked their heads at the long grey building behind them. It had once been handsome, but now it was blind, its windows boarded up, its days as a hotel long since over. Madame Gerard, still wrestling with her problems, was nowhere to be seen. I asked the men when the fair was going to be set up, and one of them looked at his watch. 'Five in the morning,' he said, and winced, shaking his hand as if he'd burned his fingers. And then it began to rain. It seemed like a good moment to duck into a bar.

I was spending the night a few kilometres away in Contrexéville. It is a town, like Vittel, almost entirely dedicated to the benefits of drinking the local spring water, and the mood of the place was appropriately sober. The sun came out again, and from the café, I could see a few couples taking their evening promenade, armed with umbrellas just in case, walking slowly and carefully on the wet pavement. The streets were clean, the trees well tended. Amazingly for France, there were none of the usual examples of imaginative parking, no cars perched on the pavement or shoehorned into alleys. A neat, quiet, orderly town, Contrexéville, the perfect setting for visitors who come not for fun and games but for the solemn purpose of bathing their innards in restorative waters.

Later, in the hotel restaurant, I witnessed a sight not often seen. In fact, it was an extraordinary sight: several dozen French couples sitting over dinner without a single bottle of wine among them. Water, water everywhere (except at my table). I was reminded of California.

The day of the fair began with a fine warm morning. Nothing moved on the streets except a cat creeping home after a disreputable night out. The rest of Contréxeville was still in bed. Evidently, drinking a great deal of water is a tiring business. When I stopped at the next village to have coffee in a sleepy café, it was a relief to stand at the bar next to a man who was enjoying a thick slice of *saucisson* with his baguette and glass of red wine for breakfast. I felt I was back in France.

I arrived in Martigny to find that it had been transformed overnight. The long, straight Rue de l'Abbe Thiébaut was packed with stands, throbbing with music, squirming with life. Behind the stands were several examples of the French genius for squeezing very large trucks into very small spaces, and from these trucks all manner of temptations had been unloaded: spicy *merguez* sausages, sugar-dusted *gaufres* (France's answer to the waffle), cages of chicks, breeding rabbits with impressive written credentials, ducks, hens, quail, guinea fowl. A trio of goats elbowed each other in a cramped pen, their mad pale eyes fixed with longing on a tantalizing display of garden plants, just out of reach on the next stand. Kits of painless face jewellery were on offer – nose studs, tongue trimmings and ear ornaments that could be stuck on rather than surgically attached. There was a name I hadn't seen before on the fashion scene, Nixon Triple Force jeans (can Clinton Executive Privilege Sportswear be far behind?). And, stacked high, their lurid colours shimmering in the sun, piles and piles of mattresses.

This puzzled me. I couldn't imagine why they were there. Why would anyone in his right mind come to a snail fair to buy a new mattress? Supposing he did, how would he get it home? And yet, even more puzzling, the mattress merchants – there were several of them competing for business – were attracting considerable interest. Knots of people stood inspecting the mattresses, leaning forward to prod them from time to time as if they were trying to awaken dormant animals. Braver souls came forward to sit down and take a test bounce. One woman was lying full length on a mattress, her shopping basket clutched to her bosom, a salesman crooning in her ear. 'Ten years of sweet dreams! Absolutely guaranteed!' For those not won over by the promise of sweet dreams, another mattress seller provided the living inducement of a reclining blonde, tightly clad in black. The crowd around her was mostly male, and rather shy. There were no prods and test bounces here.

The music was developing into a pitched battle: a traditional accordion medley coming from one stand versus Abba's Greatest Hits coming from another, with occasional fusillades of drumming booming up from the far end of the street. In a tiny garden behind one of the stands, an old lady sat on a cane chair, tapping her stick and nodding her head in time with the beat, a faint smile on her face, her slippered foot twitching. She seemed to know everybody passing by. In fact, everybody seemed to know everybody passing by, stopping for a chat, a slap on the back, a pinch of the cheek. It was more like the reunion of an enormous family than a public *fête*.

Leaving the mattresses behind, I came to a bucolic merry-go-round that might have come straight out of the Middle Ages. Four tiny ponies, no bigger than Great Danes, were clopping around in docile, patient circles, each with an appre-hensive child clinging to the reins, the mane or, in one case, a long-suffering ear. Indifferent to the noise, the heat and their escort of flies, the ponies seemed lost in their thoughts, like reluctant commuters on their way to work.

When I finally caught sight of Madame Gerard in the crowd, it was obvious from her smiling face that the problems of yesterday had been resolved. She introduced me to her mother, and they steered me to the end of the street so that I could take in every detail of the official opening ceremonies. It was important, so I was told, to observe the cutting of the ribbon and the forming up of the brass band, composed of Martigny's most accomplished musicians. And there they were, dressed in their best, with peaked hats, sky-blue jackets and white trousers. Almost hidden among the forest of legs was France's tiniest trumpeter, a boy who barely came up to the drummer's waist, his eager face several sizes too small for his peaked hat. I felt sure it would slip down over his ears as soon as he took his first energetic toot.

A nudge from Madame Gerard's mother. *Attention!* The mayor arrives, *avec son entourage.*

They provided an interesting study in sartorial styles. The mayor in his suit and tie, Miss Coquille and her two runners-up, with pale flashes of midriff showing above low-slung, snug-fitting jeans, and a clown named Pipo putting them all in the shade with his outfit of vibrant plaid trousers, plaid shoulder bag, and shiny red shoes that exactly matched his shiny red nose. He was limbering up with a few prelimi-nary capers, when the band's fanfare exploded in my ears, obliterating Abba's Greatest Hits, and the mayor stepped forward to cut the traditional tricolour ribbon stretched across the street.

The band snapped smartly into a military refrain – the march of the *escargots* – and we set off up the street, Pipo in the lead capering his heart out, followed by the band, followed by the mayor and his entourage, followed by Madame Gerard's mother and me. Madame Gerard's mother, naturally, knew everyone. This slowed us down a little, and we came to a complete stop while she persuaded her own mother to leave her garden and join the parade.

It was getting close to noon, and the warmth of the morning had turned into heat. As we made our way at a gastropod's pace up the street, I found myself taking a more than passing interest in the dim, cool rooms I could see behind the stands – rooms decorated with banners bearing pictures of smiling *escargots* and that eternally inviting word, *dégustation*. In the gloom, I was able to make out figures holding glasses. They reminded me of my mission – to meet and to eat some of the finest snails in France. Duty was calling, and it was time to get down to work.

With a final bray of brass and ruffle of drums, the procession ended at the top of the street. Making my way back, I walked into a perfumed breeze, a quiver of warm, garlic-scented air, and my nose led me to one of the *salles de dégustation*. It had probably once served as a stable, but now had been converted into a simple restaurant and bar – the walls whitewashed, the blackened tile floor polished, long wooden trestle tables and benches, a temporary kitchen set up in an alcove at the back. The menu was scrawled on a blackboard: you could have snails, snails, or snails, prepared according to your preference, with or without *frites*. There was Gewurtztraminer, chilled and spicy, to drink by the glass, by the carafe and probably by the barrel. I couldn't imagine a more pleasant working environment.

A great advantage of long tables and communal eating is enforced companionship. You might sit down alone, but solitude won't last longer than the time it takes to say *bonjour*. And, following the familiar pattern, once I admitted to being anxious for guidance and advice, someone was happy to come to my assistance.

I took my place opposite a stocky middle-aged man in a flat cap and faded shirt, his face gnarled and seasoned by the weather. He nodded amiably and asked me if I was alone. Not only was I alone, I said, but English.

'*Ah bon*?' He said he had never met an Englishman before, and he studied this novelty in silence for a few moments with a faint air of surprise. I don't know what he was expecting – a soccer hooligan, perhaps, or Major Thompson in his bowler hat – but he seemed reassured by what he saw. He offered his hand and introduced himself as Maurin, Etienne, before leaning back to take a pull at his tumbler of wine. 'You like snails?'

'I think so,' I said, 'but I haven't had them very often. I don't know anything about them.'

'Start with a dozen,' he said, 'just with garlic and butter.' He looked down at the heap of empty shells in front of him. 'I'm ready for some more myself.' He turned to call the waiter. '*Jeune homme!* An Englishman dies of hunger here.' He ordered a dozen for each of us, and a large carafe of what he called 'Gewurtz'.

Our immediate neighbours at the table were a young couple in an advanced state of romance. They were attempting the impossible – to extract flesh from hot shells, gaze into each other's eyes, and hold hands at the same time, oblivious to everything around them. They weren't going to be much use in my quest for knowledge. I turned back to my new companion and asked him to tell me what I should know about snails.

It is a perfect arrangement: a Frenchman talks, you listen. But unlike his countrymen, you don't argue with him. This is a major social asset, and you are looked upon with a measure of sympathy. You are still a foreigner, certainly, but a foreigner whose heart and stomach are in the right place, willing to sit at the feet of a master and learn about civilized matters. He, naturally, is delighted to share his superior knowledge and to air his views, *apercus*, prejudices and anecdotes to an appreciative audience.

Before Maurin had time to do much more than clear his throat and arrange his thoughts, the waiter arrived. A basket of bread and a beaded carafe were placed between us, the snails set before us, the blessing of *bon appétit* pronounced. Practical instruction could begin. Part one: how to eat a snail.

We were in a no-frills establishment. My plate was a rectangle of aluminium foil, marked with a dozen shallow indentations. Snails nestled in each of the indentations, and I could feel the heat rising from their shells. A paper napkin and a wooden toothpick completed the place setting.

The smell was glorious and I was ravenous, but my first attempt to pick up a shell ended in failure and singed fingertips. The equipment didn't run to a set of those miniature tongs supplied to snail eaters in more luxurious restaurants.

I looked across at my companion to see how he was dealing with the problem and saw an example of practical ingenuity at work in the service of the stomach. Maurin had hollowed out a slice of bread and was using the piece of crust like pincers, wrapping it around each shell so that his fingertips were insulated from the heat. With the other hand, its pinkie delicately cocked, he aimed his toothpick, stabbed, and, with a half-turn of the wrist, extracted the sizzling contents. Before putting the shell down, he raised it to his mouth and sipped the last of the juice. It all seemed terribly easy.

I imitated him as best I could, managing to extract the first snail from its shell with only minor damage to my shirtfront from an unexpected spurt of garlic butter. I looked at the object on the end of my toothpick, a dark and wrinkled morsel, not immediately appetizing, and then remembered something Régis had told me: one should eat snails through the nose, not through the eyes. They certainly smell better than they look.

The taste was better still. Snail critics – usually speaking with the conviction that is informed by considerable ignorance – will tell you to expect nothing but an aggressive rush of garlic and a mouthful of rubber, but they haven't eaten snails in Martigny. Garlic was there, of course, but it was mild and buttery and well behaved. Nor was there any hint of resistance in the flesh, which was as tender as prime steak. So far, so good. I drank the juice from the shell, mopped my chin with a piece of bread, and settled back to listen to Maurin.

He started with the nutritional news that snails are good for you, low in fat and rich in nitrogen. But – a warning finger was wagged under my nose – precautions need to be taken. Snails can thrive on a diet that would put a man in hospital; they are partial to deadly nightshade, equally deadly mush-rooms, and hemlock. Not only that. They can eat huge quantities of this fatal salad – the equivalent of half their body weight in twenty-four hours.

It wasn't the best moment to hear this, as I was halfway through my first dozen. My laden toothpick stopped in mid-air, and Maurin grinned. With these, he said, you risk nothing. They are cultivated snails, raised in an enclosed park and unable to wander; or, as he put it, to indulge their *humeur vagabonde*. Problems only arise with wild snails who can roam the fields at will, gorging on those deadly pleasures, but even these creatures can be rendered safe and delicious. All one has to do is starve them for fifteen days. At the end of the fast, each snail is carefully examined for ominous signs, then washed three times in tepid water before having its shell brushed in readiness for the oven. This is known as the *toilette des escargots.*

Surely, I said, they would be well past their best, even dead, by that time. But no. The snail can live for extended periods without food, and Maurin told me the story of a certain Monsieur Locard to prove it. It seems that Locard had invited some friends to his house for a snail feast, but he found himself with more than enough to go round. He put the surplus snails away to eat later, and for some reason which even Maurin couldn't explain, he stored them in the bottom of his wardrobe.

Time passed, and the snails were forgotten. It was not until eighteen months later when Locard, searching for something in his wardrobe, discovered his pile of shells. You and I would probably have thrown them away. Locard the optimist put them in a bucket of water and, to his astonishment, they revived.

Inspired by this tale of survival against all odds, Maurin and I ordered another dozen snails each. I was beginning to get the hang of extracting the flesh from the shell with an anticlockwise twist of the toothpick – not unlike taking the cork out of a bottle – but despite my most careful efforts to control it, the juice remained a problem. My shirt was now freckled with garlic butter, and for those of you faced with snails for the first time, I can tell you that there are only two sure ways to keep your clothes clean: nudity or a bib.

Possibly prompted by the sight of the couple next to us, who were now exchanging long, investigative kisses between snails, Maurin brought up the subject of sex. It was, as he said, the month of May, the start of the mating season, when a hermaphrodite's fancy turns to thoughts of love. And like everything else in a snail's life, this is not something to be rushed.

Maurin's hands sketched vague but suggestive intimacies in the air, his fingers weaving and then joining together, as he talked about 'preliminaries'. These can apparently last for several hours, and I couldn't help thinking that this was perhaps to give the participants time to decide on their respective genders. At any rate, once the preliminaries are out of the way, the snails copulate. *Un bon moment*, according to Maurin. Ten to fifteen days later, anything from sixty to one hundred eggs are laid. For the survivors, life expectancy can extend to six or seven years.

Maurin paused to sip his wine, and I asked the obvious question: how is it decided which of the hermaphrodite partners is female, and which is male? Telepathy? Scent? The position of the moon? Discreet horn signals? It is, after all, the most basic of the preliminaries, and if confusion occurs here it could spoil a lovely evening. Unfortunately, Maurin was unable to answer with any scientific precision. '*Ils s'arrangent*' was the best he could do. They arrange themselves.

The room was pleasantly cool. Through the doorway, the street simmered in the afternoon heat. We persuaded each other to stay inside and split another dozen. I was discovering that *escargots* are like addictive snack food; one can always find room for some more. We were eating *Gros Blancs*, or *escargots de Bourgogne*, one of the best-known among hundreds of varieties that can be found in France. Another is the smaller, less distinguished grey snail, the *Petit Gris*, and mentioning this reminded Maurin of a wicked deception.

There is, he told me, a criminal element at work in the snail world. *Tromperies*, or frauds, have been known to dupe the unsuspecting consumer, and one of the favourites is to

disguise the small grey snail as his larger and more expensive cousin. This is achieved by an imaginative system of recycling in which empty shells, once inhabited by *escargots de Bourgogne*, are re-used. Into each capacious shell is placed a *Petit Gris*, with stuffing added to take up the extra space. *Et voilá* – the customer pays for the biggest and the best, but he has been hoodwinked. It is a veritable *scandale*. And as if this weren't bad enough, one should also be aware of the menace from the East, the Chinese Connection. Maurin's face became serious, and he shook his head at the enormity of it all. Oriental molluscs, imported in industrial quantities and passed off as honest French snails!

It wasn't the first time I had heard the Chinese accused of shady practices. The truffle scam had caused a surge of out-rage, and there had been talk of Chinese attempts to infiltrate the frog market. Conveniently overlooked, of course, was the fact that foreign truffle shysters and frog smugglers need the co-operation of French partners. Imagine a salesman from Beijing, his sample case bulging with almost genuine truffles and Grade A French-type frogs. Would he pass unnoticed as he wandered through the corridors of French gastronomy? I doubt it, no matter how fluently he spoke the language.

But Chinese ingenuity didn't stop at truffles and frogs' legs. After excavating in several pockets, Maurin found a rumpled newspaper clipping that he passed across the table. 'Foie gras,' he said, in a voice laden with gloom. 'Now they're making foie gras.'

While he consoled himself with the carafe, I read the article. Two enterprising gentlemen, Mr Chan and Mr Wu, had recently set up a goose farm in the county of Hepu, just north of China's border with Vietnam. A stupendous goose farm, with a potential production capacity of more than a thousand tons a year of the real thing – goose foie gras, rather than the much more common and less expensive duck liver. This, according to the journalist's research, was nearly twice as much as current French production.

I finished reading and looked up to see Maurin shaking his head. '*Alors?*' he said, raising both hands and letting them fall to the table with a dispirited thump. 'Where will it stop?'

We were now alone at the table. Our neighbours, the lovers, had left, joined at the hip as they squeezed together through the door – on their way, I liked to think, to one of the piles of mattresses, now that they had dealt with the preliminaries over lunch. I had run out of questions, and Maurin was showing signs of fatigue brought on by Chinese infiltration and one Gewurtz too many. He was going to take a siesta before returning to the festivities. We made one of those convivial after-lunch arrangements, genuinely meant but seldom carried out, to meet at the same place the following year for another few dozen. I left him adjusting his cap against the glare of the sun, and we lurched off in opposite directions.

Back at the hotel that evening, I took from my pocket a shell I'd kept as a souvenir and washed it three times, according to correct procedure. Like my shirt, it still had a residual whiff of garlic. Looking at the shell, which was perfectly designed for its function as a mobile home and beautifully striped in shades of caramel, I wondered who had been the first human ever to peer inside such a shell at the living contents and decide that they were edible. In the raw, snails don't instantly make your mouth water. They don't have an overpoweringly appetizing smell. Their colour and texture are not to everybody's taste. And yet some brave soul took a bite and pronounced it good. Was it raging hunger, or merely curiosity?

Greeks and Romans are often given the credit for making gastronomic discoveries, but perhaps this time it was a prehistoric entrepreneur from farther east. Maybe that was it: the early, tentative stirrings of the Chinese Connection. An honourable ancestor of Mr Chan or Mr Wu, having sampled his first juicy dozen somewhere in the snail-rich fields of coastal China and finding them delicious, might have sensed an export opportunity: *Escargots de Shanghai*, preferably accompanied by a bottle of Great Wall Chinese rosé. Alas, we shall never know.

6

Undressing for lunch

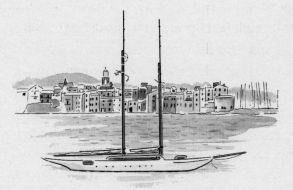

L ONG, LONG AGO, when the idle rich deserved their description and had time and servants to spare, it was customary to change for cocktails and dinner after a day of country pursuits. 'Let's get out of these wet clothes,' as Robert Benchley used to say, 'and into a dry martini.' And so damp tweeds, sodden fishing trousers, muddy plus fours, hacking jackets redolent of the stable – all were put aside, to be replaced by evening wear that had been sponged clean after the previous night's soup stains and laid out by the valet.

In due course this elitist ritual came to the attention of restaurant owners, alert, then as now, to the commercial advantages of attracting wealthy appetites. Their response – presumably an attempt to make the upper classes feel at home even when they ventured out – was to invent the restaurant dress code. It was decreed that a man should not be allowed to enjoy a meal in public unless he was properly groomed and outfitted; that is, with a suit and tie, respectable fingernails, and clean shoes.

Time passed, and standards were relaxed, although not everywhere. As we all know, many of today's more ornate and expensive restaurants still insist that their male customers wear a jacket and tie. But not, I have noticed, in France. Here, in this most fashion-conscious of countries, the clothes worn in even the best restaurants often strike the foreign visitor as surprisingly casual. Famous establishments fairly twinkling with stars, where you might expect the clients to be dressed at least as formally as the junior waiters, wouldn't dream of turning you away if you happened to show up without a tie. As for the humiliating edict that allows you through the door providing you agree to wear a borrowed tie – normally a greasy relic selected from the manager's collection of cast-offs – this is something that would never occur in a good French restaurant.

But nowhere in France has the dress code been adjusted – or indeed tossed aside altogether – with such eye-popping abandon as at Le Club 55, a restaurant on Pampelonne beach, a few kilometres south of St Tropez.

I had heard many reports about Club 55 over the years, all of them good. A place of great charm, so everyone said, where you could eat simple food and watch the boats at sea. It sounded delightful. But it was a long drive from home, and the thought of the summer traffic on the coast – often a solid, throbbing clot from Marseille to Monaco – had always put my wife and I off. Until one hot morning in July when duty called, disguised as our friend Bruno. He and his wife Janine live in the hills behind St Tropez, and they share my fondness for extended lunches.

Bruno began his phone call on a literary note. 'Still pretending to write?' he said. 'What is it this time?'

I told him I was doing research for a book that would include sections on fairs and festivals connected with food and drink, the more unusual the better. Frogs, I said, and truffles. Blood sausage, snails, tripe. That sort of thing.

'Ah,' he said, 'festivals. Well, there's a good one down here, as long as you don't mind a little bare flesh. The *fête des nanas.*'

'You mean . . .'

'Girls, my friend, girls. Girls of all ages, many of them wearing not much more than a handkerchief. A glorious sight on a sunny day. Better come soon, before the weather turns chilly and they put their clothes back on.'

Somehow it didn't sound like an event that would have an official place in guide books or calendars of cultural highlights, but it did seem worth a visit. I have known Bruno for many years, and his judgement in these matters is impeccable. 'Where does it happen?' I asked.

'Club Cinquante-Cinq, every day, except if it's raining. I don't think the girls like getting their sunglasses wet. You

really should come and do a bit of research. Never have so
many worn so little. The food's nice, too.'

Later that month, as our car crawled along behind a cara-
van on the road that corkscrews down from La Garde-Freinet
to the coast, I wondered how any establishment was able not
only to survive but to remain fashionable over several
decades. Club 55, according to the brief history Bruno had
given me, qualified as a grandfather among Riviera restaurants.

It had been started in 1955 by Genevieve and Bernard de
Colmont, whose previous claim to fame had been as pio-
neers – they were the first French people to go down the
Colorado river through the Grand Canyon by canoe.
Returning to France, they bought a patch of Pampelonne
beach. In those days, St Tropez was little more than a fishing
village with a couple of cafés, and Club 55 was little more
than a hut serving grilled sardines to friends and acquaintances of the de Colmonts. (Any strangers they didn't like,
they turned away, telling them it was a private club.) Madame
was an accomplished cook, so the menu expanded, and the
restaurant flourished, attracting a clientele that liked fresh
grilled fish and a bottle of honest rosé, with the added pleasure of eating free from the encumbrance of too many clothes.

Then, in 1956, came Brigitte Bardot, Roger Vadim, and the film that transformed St Tropez. Vadim was shooting *And God Created Woman* there, and had a film crew that, being French, would mutiny unless they were well fed. Could Madame de Colmont provide lunch every day? She did. Word spread, and, over the years, the world came. Genevieve's son Patrice took over the management of the restaurant in the mid-eighties, and he and his staff have been run off their feet every summer since.

At the time of my visit, Club 55 was in its forty-fifth year, a considerable age for any restaurant, and a near miracle considering its location and the nature of its clientele. The south of France generally, and the hyper-chic area around St Tropez in particular, doesn't seem to encourage venerable institutions. There are, of course, the old men who play *boules* outside the Colombe d'Or, the Monegasque royal family, and the casino at Monte Carlo, but they are exceptions. Change is more common, with boutiques, restaurants, hotels and night-clubs changing hands and often changing names after a few hard but lucrative years.

And who can blame the frazzled and exhausted owners for selling? Their customers, the crowds that cluster on the coast each season, are not the sweetest or best-mannered of people. In fact, if you believe half of what you hear, most of them are monsters. This is held to be true regardless of nationality, although I'm told that the Russians are now competing with the Germans, the British and even the Parisians as the least-loved visitors on the coast. 'It's not just that the Russians these days have obscene amounts of cash,' one local bar owner said. 'Nobody down here minds that. But they always look so damned *miserable*. And after a while they get drunk and start crying. It must be something in the genes.'

But it seems to me that maudlin behaviour in bars is a minor character flaw compared with some of the other vices practiced by fun-loving visitors. Arrogance, stinginess, impatience, lack of consideration, bullying, dishonesty in settling bills, petty theft (ashtrays, towels, crockery, bathrobes), the cleaning of shoes on the hotel curtains – all of these and worse make running a haven of hospitality on the Côte d'Azur a severe test of patience and restraint. And yet here was Club 55, still at it after all these years.

Turning off the narrow sandy road into the area behind the restaurant, you might imagine that you'd misread the map and ended up in California, the spiritual home of the valet parker. Young men are in attendance to save you the trouble of finding a spot for your car; young men in snappy shorts and reflective sunglasses, with the most perfect, even, burnished tans, shunting cars around with noisy nonchalance. Our elderly Peugeot was consigned to the rear of the parking area so that it wouldn't lower the tone of the front row, where a few hundred thousand dollars' worth of toys – Jaguars, Porsches and Mercedes – were cooking in the sun.

The restaurant was still only half full, but we found Janine and Bruno already installed, wine bucket at the ready. It was one o'clock – early for the real action, as Bruno said, but he thought it was important that we were well settled before the ladies began to arrive. *Les nanas*, apparently, prefer to eat a little later, and they wouldn't be in evidence much before two. So we had time to take a look at our surroundings.

What first struck me was the light, a beautiful diffused glow of sunshine filtered through bleached canvas awnings that were stretched across whitewashed wooden beams. The glow was reflected by pale-blue tablecloths, and created a most flattering effect on the complexions of the people around us. They all looked impossibly healthy. Waiters and waitresses, crisp in their whites, distributed menus and chilled bottles. Looking beyond the few stunted but tenacious trees that had taken root among the terracotta tiles between the tables, we could see the sharp, deep-blue glitter of the Mediterranean and the profile of an immense triple-decker motor yacht, doubtless with many glamorous passengers aboard. So far, so good.

Patrice stopped at our table to say hello to Janine and Bruno, and to cast a professional glance at the wine level in our glasses. Affable, worldly, relaxed, and possessed of a remarkable memory for names and faces, he must have seen the entire cast of Côte d'Azur characters come and go over the years – movie stars and politicians, financiers, gun-runners, dictators on the lam, illicit couples, dilapidated aristocrats, the models and photographers of the moment, gigolos and shady ladies. Sooner or later, they all drop in to Club 55, to look and to be looked at, sometimes hiding conspicuously behind oversized sunglasses.

Patrice wished us *bon appétit* and moved on, checking the tables, watching the staff, keeping an eye on the entrance for new arrivals, smiling, smiling. I wondered how he managed

to stay charming seven days a week throughout a long season that would inevitably include some truly poisonous customers.

'The secret is,' said Bruno, 'that it's only once a day, because they only open for lunch.' He grinned at me over the top of his menu. 'Mind you, with a bit of luck, lunch can often go on until six. What are you going to have? We'd better get the food organized before the rush.'

Mesclun and mussels and *friture* were ordered, more wine was poured. We noticed two men out on the beach, each with a cell phone, staring towards the triple-decker boat. 'Bodyguards,' said Bruno. 'They've been poking around here for half an hour, making sure there aren't any kidnappers hiding in the salad.'

We watched a speedboat set off from the mother ship, leaving a long, white-crusted curve in the water as it came towards the beach. I could make out a man standing in the stern, one hand up to his ear. What did bodyguards in these circumstances do to keep in touch before they all had cell phones – wave semaphore flags?

I turned to Janine. 'Here come the girls.'

She shook her blonde head, making those busy little clicking noises with the tongue the French love to use when you offer an opinion they don't agree with. 'You'll be lucky,' she said. 'With three bodyguards, it's much more likely to be Yeltsin's grandchildren.'

Whoever they were, it was clearly a highly valuable group of people, and the entire restaurant watched as one of the bodyguards led his precious charges to a table not far from us. Alas, despite our hopes of having exotic or celebrated neighbours, they turned out to be a perfectly normal (even if abnormally rich) American family, complete with baseball caps. Two of the bodyguards stayed out on the beach to frustrate any attempts by topless sunbathers to mount a sudden attack. The third took up his post against the wall behind us, adjusting his black belly pouch as he sat down. Weapons of one sort or another were concealed in there with the cell phone, I was sure – a few stun grenades, a baby Uzi – and I couldn't help noticing that our table was directly in the line of fire if things turned nasty and someone made moves of a threatening nature towards the baseball caps.

I was soon distracted from thoughts of perishing in the crossfire by a nudge from Janine. '*Voilà. Les mimis arrivent.*'

There were three of them, average age around twenty, swaying through the tables on the platform-soled shoes that were the fad of the season. Their tans were of the luminous, well-established kind – impossible to achieve in the course of a normal vacation – that require many weeks of judicious oiling and broiling. One had the feeling that even the crevices between the girls' toes would be the same dark caramel colour as their long legs, their fashionably concave stomachs, and their jaunty, high-slung bosoms. They had all made the same gesture towards modesty by draping flimsy, brightly coloured pareos around their hips. But by some extraordinary mischance these had become damp on the way to the restaurant, and clung like another skin to every cleft and declivity they were supposed to conceal.

'Did you see the girl at the back?' Bruno asked. 'I swear her sunglasses were bigger than her bra.' He looked towards the entrance. 'I wonder where the wallets are.'

In fact, the nubile trio were making do with a single companion, an older, leathery man with a grizzled froth of chest hair escaping from an unbuttoned shirt. He settled himself among his girls, arranging his lunchtime essentials on the table – cigarettes, gold lighter, and cell phone – before reaching over to pinch the cheek of one of the *mimis*.

Janine sniffed. 'Their uncle, of course.' It takes a Frenchwoman to recognize these distant family connections.

By now, there was a continuous flurry of new arrivals, cruising the tables to greet long-lost acquaintances, some of whom they hadn't seen since dinner the previous night. The air was loud with chirrups of joyful surprise – '*Tiens! C'est toi!*' – and the moist little smack of social kisses. The festival of *nanas* was warming up, and it was possible to identify two distinct generations by their choice of clothing. For the young: vestigial bikinis (baseball caps optional), shorts trimmed off to just this side of decency, revealing a hint of the lower curve of the buttock, and T-shirts worn as dresses. The more mature ladies were almost discreet by comparison: sarongs, silk shirts, gauzy transparent trousers – in some cases rather too transparent – profound cleavage and emphatic jewellery. There were also some interesting examples of the cosmetic surgeon's art to be seen, and we were fortunate in having an expert to instruct us in the finer points.

Janine, although unlifted herself, says she can spot *le lifting* from a distance of twenty paces. Why, only the other night she had been at a dinner party where three of the guests, one a man, were displaying what she called 'signature lifts'. All three of them, she could tell, had been performed by the same surgeon.

I wondered if he actually did sign his work. And if so, where? And how? A maker's mark under the left breast? A monogram behind one ear? An actual signature, even, somewhere on the downy reaches of the upper thigh? With status labels being so popular these days, it wouldn't have surprised me. But it's nothing as crude as that, apparently; it's more a question of individual style, not unlike the distinctive cut of a couturier. Cosmetic surgery has its Diors and Chanels, and when looking at a suspiciously taut and chiselled jawline or an artfully hoisted bust, the informed eye can often identify who did what.

With some women, the urge to tinker with nature turns into the hobby of a lifetime, and what started as a minor nip and tuck around the eyelids is extended downward, until very little remains of the original bodywork. Janine told us of one legendary fixture on the Côte d'Azur each summer (her winters were spent under the knife and in recovery) who had been lifted so many times and in so many places that when she smiled, the skin on the backs of her ankles could be seen to tighten and twitch upward.

'There's another one who's overdone it,' said Janine, nodding towards a woman of a certain age who had stopped on the way to her table for a chat with some friends. 'Watch when she lifts her arms.' I watched as the woman raised her arms to tuck a few tendrils of hair behind her ears. 'See? *C'est la poitrine fixée*. The breasts don't move. They have been anchored like buttons on a waistcoat.'

I don't think I ever would have noticed. But once it was pointed out to me, I found the phenomenon fascinating, and had to force myself to look away. 'It's terrible,' I said to Bruno. 'I can't stop staring.'

He shrugged. 'Why do you think she had it done? Nobody comes here to be ignored. It's a show. The bodies are here to be looked at.' And he went on to tell us of an incident that illustrated his point.

A lovely and amply endowed young woman discovered, in the course of a particularly animated conversation, that one breast had managed to slip out of the top of her swimsuit. She could quite easily and unobtrusively have slipped it back, but instead let out a piercing '*Ooh-la-la!*' This, of course, had the desired effect, attracting the attention of all those at the neighbouring tables, who were then treated to the sight of the young woman seeming to have an enormous problem – a *crise de sein* – persuading the playful breast back into the swimsuit from which it had escaped. One of the gentleman spectators, sympathetic to her difficulties, was heard to call out, 'Waiter! Bring the lady two large spoons!' He then added a considerate afterthought. 'And be a good fellow – make sure the spoons are warm, will you?'

On paper, the story seems extremely unlikely. And yet, surrounded as we were by an exhibition of near nudity, it was easy enough to imagine that it had happened. Nobody, or at least none of the women, had dressed to avoid being noticed. Inevitably, there were one or two cases where optimism had triumphed over age, and the desire to create a striking effect had been somewhat misjudged. The leopard print swimsuit worn with a black mesh miniskirt was one example; a pair of see-through floral print tights was another. Both outfits were worn by women long past the bloom of youth, and looking up at them from a seated position – seeing the involuntary judder of flesh as they passed – one was aware of that old enemy, gravity. But, as so often with French women, these two had refused to acknowledge the passage of time. In their hearts they were stars of the beach, confident of their eternal allure, and had dressed accordingly.

It was noticeable that while all the ladies had made an effort that day, many of their escorts hadn't bothered. The men, for the most part, were not a pretty sight. Some of them – I imagine they were off-duty captains of industry – wouldn't have qualified sartorially to get a job as a *plongeur*, or dishwasher in the kitchen, let alone as a waiter. They appeared to have slept in their rumpled shorts and scruffy shirts. Their hair was lank and uncombed. They radiated neglect – but a self-satisfied neglect, as if to tell the world that they were important enough not to have to bother with their appearance. They were not a credit to their companions.

The standard improved around three o'clock, with an influx of older gentlemen and their consorts. There was a faded, salty elegance to their yachting clothes, a notable and welcome absence of the logos and nautical trimmings that make many of today's sailors look as though they've been gift-wrapped. Even more impressive, the new arrivals had come from their boats all by themselves, without the benefit of bodyguards, and didn't seem to possess cell phones. They were a breath of nostalgia, and might almost have stepped out of one of Sara and Gerald Murphy's 1920s house parties, leaving Scott Fitzgerald and Hemingway behind to drink and hurl sentences at each other.

Our waiter, a young man with the foresight to anticipate a wine crisis, slipped a full bottle into the ice bucket and asked if we might like some *fraises des bois* after the cheese. We took a break from the people and allowed ourselves to be distracted by the food.

To be consistently successful, beach cuisine should be informal, fresh and uncomplicated. A sandy kitchen is no place for a chef who likes to drown his fish in sauces, or to punctuate the course of a meal with a flourish of herbal sorbets and pastry-wrapped titbits. These might all be fine in grand restaurants, but not here. Sitting with your shoes kicked off under the table, you should be able to taste the sea as well as look at it. Back to nature, even if the parking lot is stuffed with Maseratis.

Simplicity and freshness have been part of the formula at Club 55, and they are clearly two of the reasons for its enduring success. The fish, the vegetables and the salads are the way they should be, fresh enough to stand up for themselves without any assistance from over-enthusiastic seasoning. And the *pommes frites* have the satisfying texture that comes from two immersions in hot oil – the first to cook the interior, the second for a crisp outer coating. Anyone looking for a good lunch won't be disappointed.

A good lunch, however – mere food – is a bonus, only part of the experience. The meal over, but with a ferocious jolt of espresso as an excuse to linger, there is nothing to divert your attention from the *après*-lunch stirrings that are starting to take place around you. A middle-aged man wearing denim and bright red spectacles, with a crash helmet dangling from one hand, makes his way through the crowd with a slightly anxious expression, as though his bike has wandered off without him. Two tables from us, a future *nana*, very young, very beautiful, very bored, sits with her parents practising her sultry expression on passing waiters. Dogs no bigger than handbags are lifted on to laps and given almond biscuits. It's four o'clock, and the rest of the world is working, a thought that contributes to the agreeable air of decadence that has now descended on the restaurant.

Table-hoppers resume their hopping, but not with the same nimble eagerness they showed earlier. Made languid by lunch, they saunter over for guest appearances at other tables, there to perch and have lengthy discussions about what to do with the remainder of the afternoon. But it seems that even lotus-eaters have their problems. Eavesdropping reveals that water-skiing plays havoc with the digestion, that sunbathing is not recommended for the skin. (This comment sounds odd, coming as it does from a cocoa-coloured *mimi*.) Fortunately for those in need of something to fill those long hours between lunch and dinner, shopping has not so far revealed any serious health hazards. And Club 55 has thoughtfully provided its own boutique, only a short stagger away, along the beach. We decide to have a look.

In its own highly relaxed way, the trip of a hundred metres or so from the restaurant to the boutique is a model of ingenious design and sophisticated retail psychology. I think it has been based on the assumption that most men detest shopping for women's clothes. They don't have the aptitude for it, and they are pathetically lacking in stamina. They flag easily, and then they mope, and finally they drag their unwilling companions away, leaving the premises only partly ransacked. This unprofitable condition – purchase *interruptus* – has been anticipated by the people at Club 55, who have installed, on the way to the boutique, two rest areas where the reluctant but occasionally useful masculine accessory can take his ease and enjoy the scenery.

The first stop is a bar, ideally placed to appeal to those who have forgotten to have an after-lunch *digestif*. Dress seems to be even more optional than in the restaurant, and swimsuits more vestigial, although this may be because the bodies are fully visible and no longer partly obscured by restaurant tables. In any case, shoppers can park their companions here, secure in the knowledge that for at least half an hour they will be pleasantly diverted.

A few metres further on is an outdoor seating area, with long couches facing the sea. On the day we were there, it had been almost completely taken over by men with not a second to waste away from the pursuit of money and the conduct of their businesses. Oblivious to the glories of nature spread out before them (some of whom were wearing very little more than a coating of oil), the men were bellowing instructions to some distant office, to their yacht captains, to their brokers, to their real estate agents. There is something about cell phones – I have yet to find out what it is – that compels callers to raise their voices, so that anyone nearby is obliged to hear details of their private conversations. This has become an almost inescapable nuisance, and I look forward to the day when cell phone addicts, like smokers, are herded together and sent into exile. Preferably in a soundproof room.

In contrast to the babble on the beach, the loudest sounds in the boutique were the swish of plastic and the whisper of banknotes changing hands. Figures in varying stages of undress flitted in and out of the changing cabin. Sales were brisk. Men were scarce. They would be picked up later, festooned with shopping bags, and led away to whatever joys awaited them that evening.

But first, there would be the car to fetch, and it was not always the uncomplicated business one might expect. As we walked back along the beach, with the sun starting to descend for its evening dip into the sea, Bruno told me about the man – one of those slightly seedy captains of industry – who had been waiting while the valet parker was fetching his Bentley. A young couple then arrived in the parking area. Seeing nobody else, the young man went up to the captain of industry and pressed a fifty-franc note into his hand. 'Mine's the banana-yellow Ferrari over there,' he said. 'Mind you don't scratch it.'

One can only imagine the poor man's feelings. Revered by his secretary, respected by financial analysts, treated with deference by all around him, he had clambered to the giddy heights of corporate success, only to be mistaken for a parking lot cowboy. The horror of it! In fact, as Bruno pointed out, the valet parkers are much better dressed than he was, but that kind of detail is easy to miss after a long lunch.

As my wife and I were getting close to home the next morning, we noticed that everyone in the village was fully dressed. When we got to the house, I had to park the car without professional assistance. We were greeted by dogs who have never sat on laps in restaurants and a guest who told us that the plumbing had started to make mysterious noises. Our short break from real life was over.

7

Love at first sniff

Contrary to popular belief, the way to a man's heart is not necessarily through his stomach. His nose can be equally susceptible, and for proof, one has to look no further than my friend Sadler. Like me, he is an Englishman who has chosen to live in France. Like me, he is a writer. And like me, he has a weakness for all things French, particularly those that come in a glass or on a plate.

Our story starts in the port of Dieppe. The cross-channel ferry had just docked after arriving from England, and a tall, purposeful figure hurried down the gangplank. It was Sadler, delighted to be back in his adopted country and in the mood to celebrate. But how, and with what? Striding through the streets of Dieppe, stomach rumbling gently, his eye was caught by a voluptuous display of cheeses – a bevy of them, reclining, nude – in the window of an *épicerie fine*. The rumble rose to a crescendo. Feeling an overwhelming desire for a true taste of France, he decided to investigate.

There are, so they say, more cheeses in France than there are days in the year – every texture from crumbly to almost liquid, every degree of flavour from razor-sharp to the subtle mildness of cream, cheeses from cows, goats and ewes, cheeses seasoned with herbs, prickled with pepper, marinated in olive oil, aged on beds of rushes. To choose a single cheese from among hundreds is, for most of us, one of life's minor challenges.

But not for Sadler; or at least, not this time. Once inside the shop, his nose began to browse through the invisible but aromatic mist that hung above the assembled cheeses. Head lowered, eyes half-closed, nostrils a-quiver, he found himself drawn as if by destiny itself towards a particularly assertive bouquet. It came from a plump disc, rusty orange in colour, its ample girth contained by five bands of sedge grass: a cheese from Livarot, known to its admirers as *le colonel* (because of the five stripes), and reputed to be one of the most pungent cheeses in the world.

Sadler fell in love. He bought the cheese, took it out to lunch, and then travelled with it in his car all the way home to Paris. *Le colonel* made its presence increasingly felt with every passing kilometre, but it was music to Sadler's nose, and it may even have inspired the fantasy that we will come to later.

Last year, this encounter with the cheese was recorded in a memoir Sadler wrote about his experiences as an Englishman living in Paris, and it wasn't long before he received a phone call from Livarot. A gentleman highly placed in the local cheese hierarchy had read the book, and he was delighted to discover someone who was such an outspoken supporter of Livarot's pride and joy. And since the book had been written in French and had appeared on the French best-seller lists, nationwide publicity for the town was assured. It was a coup for Livarot, and one that deserved official recognition. Nothing less than the highest honour would do. Would the amiable Monsieur Sadler agree to be the sponsor of the annual Livarot cheese fair, and become a specially elected *chevalier de fromage*?

How could he refuse? To be rewarded for eating is a dream that comes true for very few of us, and Sadler was quick to accept. He called me with the news.

'It's the cheese Hall of Fame,' he said. 'I'm getting a medal. The town will spend the whole weekend celebrating. The streets will be running with wine and Livarot. Pack your bags. I need you there to hold my coat.'

Which is how I found myself on a hot Saturday afternoon in August driving past the half-timbered houses and endless orchards of the Normandy countryside. This region of France, padded with green fields, rich in cows and apples, steeped in cream and Calvados, was the home of the warriors who invaded England under William the Conqueror. (A man who, despite his aggressive behaviour, was evidently a caring and generous father. When he died in 1087, he left Normandy to his eldest son, Robert. To another son, William Rufus, he bequeathed England. Luckily for the boys, there were no inheritance taxes in those days.)

The current invasion is coming the other way, with the English settling in to Norman farms and manor houses, bringing with them their marmalade and their addiction to those indispensable aids to civilization, British newspapers. As I walked down the crowded main street of Livarot, I heard an English voice – a loud, peevish English voice – complaining about the price the local newsagent had just charged for yesterday's edition of *The Times*. Somehow, I couldn't imagine a Frenchman in a small English country town complaining about the price of *Le Monde*. But then, he would never be able to find a copy of *Le Monde* in a small English country town. We remain an insular bunch. The ghost of my old boss Jenkins is with us yet.

I had been told to meet Sadler in the hotel at the bottom of the main street. Knowing my man, I made for the hotel restaurant, and there he was, still at the table, preparing himself for greatness with a final glass of wine and scribbling on the back of an envelope.

'I thought I ought to give a speech,' he said, tapping the envelope. 'Here' – he pushed a sheet of yellow paper across the table – 'take a look at the programme while I finish my notes.' He resumed scribbling. I studied the sheet.

Everything one could hope to find at a cheese fair of this importance was there: an *apéritif concert*, a marching band, cheese tastings, cider tastings, Calvados tastings, barbecue stands, a fairground and a grand Saturday night ball. There were, as well, two other attractions I hadn't been expecting. That very afternoon, there was to be a sealed bid auction of forty *amouillantes*, or cows that were in calf. And the following afternoon, a speed-eating competition under strict Livarot rules to establish who could consume the most cheese in a specified time period and take the title of *le plus gros mangeur*.

Sadler finished his notes with a flourish of the pen. 'There. I'm the event that comes after the pregnant cows,' he said. 'And when the ceremony's finished we're going to do a little work. A book-signing.'

'We are?'

'Certainly. We'll be at a table just up the street, with full authors' comforts, choice of cider or wine. It's all arranged. You'll love it.'

Before I had a chance to reply, one of the fair's official organizers arrived to make sure Sadler was ready for his moment of glory, or to restrain him from ordering another bottle of wine. I wasn't sure which. The future *chevalier de fromage* allowed himself to be led away, and I decided to pay my respects to motherhood: a quiet interlude among the cows was necessary before the high drama of the afternoon's main event.

I like cows. There is something very soothing about them. It is rare to see them hurry. At a distance, they radiate serenity, moving slowly, tails flicking, placid and picturesque. At close quarters, you notice their eyelashes, the steady oval motion of their jaws as they chew their cud, and, usually, the fact that they are caked in muck from chest to hoof. These cows, however, had come straight from the bovine beauty parlour. They were arranged in a long, immaculate line, groomed to a whisker. Their tan-and-cream coats gleamed, their hooves were buffed to a dark sheen, their eyes were bright. Pregnancy agreed with them.

Except for the rustle of envelopes containing the bids, the auction had been silent. The cows were silent. The spectators were silent. Livarot seemed set for a drowsy afternoon. And then the peace was broken by the burp of a microphone and

a rasp of amplified throat-clearing. I followed the sounds to the Place Pasteur, where Sadler was to be immortalized, and was nearly run over by a flying wedge of *confrères* making their way through the crowd. Wearing cloaks and hats of brown velvet, medals twinkling in the sun, they mounted the steps of a raised platform and formed into ranks on either side of the lady mayor of Livarot and the lone Englishman.

Far from looking nervous, Sadler was pawing the ground in anticipation, chatting to everyone within earshot, waving regally to the audience, a man poised for stardom and enjoying every minute of it.

A cloaked figure stepped forward and took the microphone, notes at the ready, to introduce the new *chevalier* to the world. According to tradition, a suitable introduction on these occasions, as was the case in Vittel, is a mixture of praise and scurrilous indiscretion. Knowing Sadler as I did, I thought that the assassination of his character might easily stretch into the early evening. But for some reason he was allowed to escape with only a few minor scars to his reputation – trifling sins that wouldn't even make the pages of the local newspaper – and then we were ready for the rites of initiation.

Sadler was given a wedge of Livarot, a large wedge, but a mere nothing for a man of his infinite capacity; it disappeared in seconds. He was then given a goblet, more a bucket than a glass, containing enough Normandy cider to put out a small fire. Here was a challenge that would separate the men from the boys. The crowd fell silent as the goblet was raised. To Sadler's great credit, considering the food and wine he had already demolished at lunch, he drained the goblet in one prolonged, open-throated swallow. The crowd showed its appreciation: whistles, applause, exclamations of *ooh-la-la*! The *confrères* were visibly impressed. Our hero had earned his medal.

Sadler's wife Lulu was standing next to me. 'He did very well,' I said to her.

She nodded. '*C'est normal*. I have never known him to fail with a glass.'

With the opening formalities over, the crowd settled down to listen to the acceptance speech. Had it been me, this ordeal would have been over in less time than it takes to eat a piece of cheese: a muttered thank you, most kind, highly honoured, off we go. But Sadler is made of more discursive stuff. Between meals, he is a university lecturer, which must help.

Also, his French is perfect. And, of course, he had a skinful of cider inside him. At any rate, he seized the microphone with such eagerness that I thought he was going to take a bite out of it.

With his opening remarks, he showed himself to be an accomplished speaker with a nicely judged sense of what would appeal to his audience. 'I have a fantasy,' he said. 'It is to make love to my wife on a mattress made entirely of Livarot cheese.' Lulu bowed her head. Being a Frenchwoman of considerable refinement, she prefers to keep the door of the boudoir closed. But there was no stopping Sadler now that he was in the bedroom. 'I shall wear my medal in bed tonight,' he promised. What a picture that conjured up. And with the audience hanging on his every word, he continued to discuss sex, cheese, literature, and his love of France – or perhaps he called it lust – for several rousing minutes before moving on to his finale.

Without giving up the microphone, he pounced on the lady mayor and kissed her. Then he kissed the other female members of the *confrérie*. Then, with a cry of 'I'm English, so I'm allowed to kiss the men,' he nuzzled each of his *confrères*. Imagine a politician in heat at election time, and there you have it. The moist smack of each kiss, picked up by the microphone and amplified through the speakers, echoed across the square. '*Mon Dieu*,' said an admiring voice in the crowd, 'how they have changed, the English, since the departure of Madame Thatcher.' And I had to sit at a table with this man and sign books.

Fortunately, a determined official had managed to extract

the microphone from Sadler's grip before we reached the table, frustrating his hopes of broadcasting promotional announcements for the signing. We placed our orders for drinks, settled down behind piles of our books, and waited to be overwhelmed by an adoring public.

It is a curious and often humbling experience to be an author on these occasions; not unlike being an exhibit in a zoo. People gather just out of conversational range and stare at you. You attempt what you hope to be an inviting smile. They take one pace backwards, still staring. You pick up the odd comment: '. . . He's older than he looks in his photograph . . . I think I'll wait for the paperback to come out . . . They're all on the bottle, you know, those writers . . . I feel sorry for his wife . . . Go on, you ask him.' Ask him what? You long to be asked something, anything, to relieve your lonely vigil. But the question seldom comes. One intrepid soul, braver than the rest, approaches the table, picks up your book, flicks through the pages, puts it down, and retreats without once looking directly at you. It is as if you are a human dump bin.

Not this time, though. Not in the company of a medal-wearing celebrity, the *chevalier* Sadler, still glowing with the after-effects of applause and high-octane cider. We passed an entertaining and convivial hour, signed some books, and found the people of Livarot to be enormously, wonderfully jolly. Great kissers, too. I've always believed that colder climates breed colder personalities, and that the farther north one goes, the more reserved people become. But here we saw many examples of lengthy embraces punctuated by four kisses, double the normal French ration. I noticed that this seemed to cause Sadler some concern, and it turned out he was worried he might have short-changed his *confrères* on the platform; might, indeed, have made himself appear to be suffering from English *froideur*. 'I think I may have underkissed them,' he said. 'But I'll make up for it tonight at the dinner.'

The weather continued to be kind to us. All of Livarot seemed to be out on the town that evening, sauntering through streets that smelled of meat grilling on barbecues, of pancakes like golden cobwebs spread out on flat cast-iron skillets, of toasting cheese, of cider. We passed a brazier sizzling with *andouillette* – small, potent sausages stuffed with tripe – and I saw the Sadler nostrils begin to fibrillate. 'I could murder a couple of those,' he said. 'It seems an awfully long time since lunch.' He adjusted his medal and quickened his pace as we turned off the main street and into the *place* where dinner was being served.

It was a *repas campagnard*, an informal buffet. Under a canvas awning, long tables had been set out, lighted from above by a string of bare forty-watt bulbs. The effect was a particular kind of glow that I always associate with France, not quite dim, but certainly far from bright; a summer glow, evocative of long warm evenings spent out of doors, wine bottles on plank tables, the flutter of moths overhead. I mentioned this to Sadler, normally a man of great aesthetic sensibilities, but his mind was elsewhere, his eye fixed firmly on the buffet.

Generous was the word for it: hams, sausages, flans, quiches, salads as big as landscapes, monumental bowls of potatoes *à la mayonnaise* and – of course – wall-to-wall cheeses: there was Livarot ('the working man's meat'), Camembert, Pont l'Eveque, Pavé d'Auge. We filled our plates and found our places at a table for twelve. Although the *bon-homie* was deafening, I could tell that I had somehow caused offense to the woman sitting opposite me. She was peering at what I had on my plate, and it obviously displeased her. Looking up at me, she cocked her index finger and began to wag it, a sure sign that I had done something unspeakable.

'Monsieur! You have no cheese!'

It was true; my plate was full, but for the moment cheese-less. I was planning to go back for some. Before I had a chance to explain, though, madame leaned forward to make sure I could hear what came next.

'Let me tell you what the great Brillat-Savarin once said: "A meal without cheese is a beautiful woman without one eye." *Voilà, monsieur.*'

I looked around for my *chevalier* friend to rescue me, but he was busily engaged kissing someone at the next table. Lulu was too far away to help. I would have to deal with my accuser by myself. Later, I promised her, I would attack the cheese. And speaking of attacking cheese, would madame be kind enough to tell me about tomorrow's eating competition – the rules of the game, techniques, contestants. Was there a favourite? Could one bet?

This prompted others at the table to join the conversation, with the usual barrage of conflicting opinions. However, it was generally agreed that there was a favourite, a local man who had triumphed in previous years. The rumour was that he'd been training hard and was in top form. *Mais attention!*

There was also an exotic outsider, a dark horse who was coming all the way from Clermont-Ferrand, in the middle of France. A woman. Not only that, but a Japanese woman. This was the cause of considerable satisfaction around the table, confirming as it did the *renommée mondiale* of Livarot and its cheese.

By now, madame had assumed responsibility for the rest of my meal. Seeing that I had cleared a space on my plate, she escorted me back to the buffet to supervise the selection of cheese. I picked out what I thought was a good-sized triangle of Livarot. Madame clucked her tongue in disapproval. I was being too restrained. She prodded some larger pieces with a knowledgeable finger to test for ripeness, chose one of the biggest, and added it to my plate.

Livarot is not a modest cheese. It announces itself to the nose long before it is anywhere near your mouth, with a piercing, almost astringent aroma. It is dense, chewy, elastic, creamy, brimming with fat (45 per cent) and altogether deli-cious – about as far away as it's possible to get from those bland, overprocessed dollops that call themselves cottage cheese. Madame watched me while I ate, nodding with satis-faction. By the time my Livarot was finished, so was I. My forehead was covered in a light sweat; heart palpitations would surely follow. But madame hadn't done with me yet.

'*Bien*,' she said. 'Now what you need is a little Calvados, to settle the digestion.'

Sadler, whose ears are as highly tuned and sensitive as a bat's to certain stimuli, had heard the magic word. His diges-tion (that poor long-suffering process) would also be greatly

improved, he said, by a nightcap. And, as he pointed out, the Normans invented Calvados. If only for reasons of politeness towards our hosts, we should follow madame's advice.

And so we did, sitting around the kitchen table in a house belonging to a hospitable member of the organizing committee. A dark, anonymous bottle was produced: unlabelled, undated, homemade Calvados, with a bouquet that bought tears to the eyes, a roundness that filled the mouth, a smooth warmth that spread from throat to stomach. 'Internal sunshine,' they call it. That night I slept like a stump.

One of the many pleasant unfairnesses of life is the unexpectedly benign way in which the body sometimes reacts to excess. I deserved a hangover. Sadler deserved far worse. And yet, the following morning, we both felt remarkably well; rested, refreshed, ready for the events of the day, even if they included, as they inevitably would, cheese and Calvados. We left the hotel and went in search of coffee.

Although it was only a little after ten o'clock, the braziers in the main street were already lighted; beside them, long necklaces of sausage were arranged in glistening coils the colour of blood. The dog population of Livarot was out in force, loitering with intent and trying to look innocent, hoping that a back would be turned long enough to allow a lightning sausage raid. Walking through town, we kept coming across trucks that had turned themselves into restaurants – side panels lowered to reveal minuscule bars, awnings put up, chairs and tables set out on the street, good smells coming from handkerchief-sized kitchens. Sadler looked at his watch, decided that even for him it was too early for lunch, and then suddenly stopped, his medal bouncing against his chest. He had noticed something fascinating on the far side of the Place Pasteur.

He took me by the elbow. 'Do you see what I see?'

It was a small stand, almost entirely taken up by barrels and a bar. Men with vividly tinted noses were nursing snifters or plastic tumblers, looking pensive. On the awning, those fateful words: *Dégustation Cidre et Calvados*.

Sadler's face was the picture of innocence. 'It's only apples,' he said, 'and you can always spit it out.'

I looked at Lulu. She smiled and nodded. What could I do?

In fact, mid-morning is an excellent time to *déguster*. Breakfast is a distant memory, lunch is still to come, the eye is bright, and the palate is clean and undistracted. We lined up at the bar, wondering whether there were more vitamins in cider or in Calvados. Both would have to be tried.

Although cider is not one of my favourite drinks, there was no denying that this was a prime drop. There was a freshness about it, and a powerful, heady taste of the fruit. They say that pigs and horses fortunate enough to live in Normandy frequently get tipsy on fallen apples that have started to ferment. And we were told of Gaston *le picoleur*, the alcoholic pig, so fond of his fix that he used to go around the orchard butting trees to make the apples fall. So much for the gentle pleasures of cider.

We moved on to what our new friend behind the bar called 'the reason God created apples'. Calvados of varying ages – from *jeune homme* to *grandpère* – was poured, inhaled, sipped, and, I must confess, swallowed. Strangely enough, I had no problem at all drinking 84-proof alcohol before midday; no wincing, no shakes, no burning sensations. Perhaps last night's cheese was still protecting my vital organs with a layer of insulation. We decided to buy a couple of bottles of Calvados to take home for future reference, and then Lulu very wisely suggested more coffee.

Our arrival at the café coincided with the first musical interlude of the day. The official Livarot cheese fair band was snaking down the main street playing very accomplished jazz, led by the *chef d'orchestre*, a large man with an impressively supple touch on the trumpet; ornamental riffs worthy of Miles Davis.

The band came to a stop in the square and put aside jazz to reach deep into its repertoire for something completely different. They began to play. Unless my ears were deceiving me, the first few notes sounded exactly like the start of 'It's A Long Way To Tipperary', which is somehow not what you would expect to hear in rural France. And yet that's what it turned out to be. Naturally, the performance had been given a little Norman *je ne sais quoi*, and it was, appropriately, a long way from the conventional rendition I remembered from my boyhood. The instrumental arrangement, with its jaunty swoops and flourishes, reminded me more of New Orleans

than of a military march. And the band sang the words, giving
a completely new sound to the destination: '*Eets a longwhy to
Teeppairairee* . . .' The crowd loved it; encores were demanded,
and in the course of the next few hours we were to hear the
song several more times.

A cheese stand opposite the café had appeared on Sadler's
radar screen, luring him away for a swift, decisive visit to
buy supplies to take back to Paris. He returned to the café
looking thoughtful. The sight of a panorama of Livarot spread
across the stand had reminded him of the afternoon's competition. How do you get ready for something like that?

We tried to imagine the regime of self-denial, the months
of struggle and sacrifice, the preparations required to bring a
competitor to peak condition before a concentrated onslaught
of cheese and cider. Fasting? Calisthenics? Jogging around
town? Meditation? Colonic irrigation? Stomach massage? In
the end, Lulu's suggestion – the French answer to circuit
training – was probably the one followed by most of the competitors. 'Lunch,' she said, 'but only a light lunch.'

'What a good idea,' said Sadler.

Three o'clock, and a long table had been set up on the
platform in the Place Pasteur. As a warm-up act before the
featured competition, some twisted genius had devised a special contest for the younger gourmet. Children were lined up
at the table in teams of two, one sitting, one standing behind.
The one standing behind (the feeder) had to spoon yoghurt
into the mouth of his or her seated teammate (the eater).
Simple enough, except that the feeders all had black plastic
bags over their heads, and so had to locate the eaters' mouths

blind: by touch, trial, and messy error. The *animateur*, a young man with a microphone, a breathless line of non-stop patter, and an acrobatic ability to dodge flying gobs of yoghurt, supervised the proceedings. After ten minutes, all the children and most of the table had been covered with a coating of white goo. Everyone agreed that the event had been an outstanding success.

After some swabbing down by the hygiene squad, table and chairs were ready for the *grands mangeurs*, and one by one these Olympians of gluttony – nine of them – came up to take their places. There was much applause from the crowd, particularly for the favourite, a surprisingly slim man. And a real ovation for the Japanese dark horse from Clermont-Ferrand, Mademoiselle Iku, a small, slender young lady who looked as though she would have difficulty dealing with a baguette, let alone a couple of pounds of Livarot. The *animateur* asked her how she felt. She giggled and waved to the crowd. 'She's confident, that one,' said someone behind me. 'She has *beaucoup d'élan*. But does she have the stomach for cheese?'

The *animateur* explained the rules. There was a time limit of fifteen minutes, during which contestants had to eat their way through two entire cheeses. Each cheese weighed nine hundred grams, or about two pounds. Liquid assistance was available in the form of bottles of cider. Any attempts to secrete cheese in the clothing would be punished by disqualification. May the best mouth win.

The favourite could be seen warming up, flexing his jaw muscles and rolling his shoulders, eyeing his opponents, taking the cap off his bottle of cider. He was asked what he had done that day in the way of last-minute training. As Lulu had predicted, he said he had made do with a light lunch. Next question: how often did he eat cheese? Once a year, he said. End of interview. He refused to be drawn out, clearly saving himself for the supreme effort to come.

And they're off! All nine of them make a strong start, tearing at their cheese like dogs savaging a postman's trousers. It's a brutal pace. It can't possibly last; this is a marathon, not a sprint. After two or three minutes, the contestants settle down to a less frenzied rhythm, and the differences in their techniques begin to show themselves. You can tell the first-time competitors by the uneven size of their mouthfuls, a certain lack of smoothness in their arm movements, and their tendency to glance sideways to see how their opponents are doing. A great mistake, or so we're informed by an expert standing close by, the cheese-eating equivalent of taking your eye off the ball.

Two different and distinctly superior styles are now apparent. There is the Zen of Mademoiselle Iku, her gaze focused on some inspirational sight in the far distance as she chews and swallows at a steady pace, wiping her lips delicately between mouthfuls with a paper napkin, taking ladylike sips of cider. If there were a special prize for the most graceful consumption of an indecent amount of Livarot, she would walk away with it.

By way of contrast, there are the no-holds-barred tactics of the champ. He takes double bites, double mouthfuls, stuffing one mouthful in each cheek, leaving just enough space in the middle of his mouth to allow the passage of a torrent of cider that swills the cheese down his gullet. The man is like a machine, eating rind and all, mopping his brow, signalling for another bottle of cider. There can be no doubt about it. We are in the presence of cheese-eating greatness here. '*Quel mec!*' cries one of his fans. '*Il est formidable.*' What a guy. And what a digestive system.

With a final double mouthful, a last huge swig of cider, and a well-earned belch, the favourite finishes, raising both arms in a victory salute. He has eaten four pounds of cheese and drunk one and a half litres of cider in twelve minutes flat. This may be a world record. Sweating profusely, he stands up – in itself a small miracle – to be interviewed by the *animateur*.

'Congratulations! How does it feel to win again?'

'*Génial.* No more cheese for a year.'

End of interview. The champion is a man of few words. Or perhaps he has a surfeit of Livarot wrapped around his vocal chords.

The *animateur* moves on to Mademoiselle Iku, who has acquitted herself with considerable distinction, having consumed two pounds of cheese and a bottle of cider without any visible distress. In between giggles, she tells us that she loves cheese, and that Livarot is ten times more expensive in Tokyo than it is in France. She is presented with a special trophy for the best female performance, and a replica, in chocolate, of a Livarot *colonel*.

Other contestants show the strain of pushing their bodies to inhuman limits in the cause of sporting endeavour. Some slump over the table, heads resting on their arms, breathing heavily, barely this side of consciousness; others are draped like sacks across the backs of their chairs, arms hanging down, faces as pale as Camembert, glistening with sweat. And they say professional boxing is tough; they should try competitive cheese-eating. We leave the exhausted *mangeurs* to recover, and walk back towards the distant strains of 'It's A Long Way To Tipperary' coming from the main street.

What a grand time we've had. Rations, company, entertainment, weather, the warmth of the Livarot welcome – everything has conspired to make the weekend memorable. And it has reminded me that there's nobody – not even Régis – who is Sadler's equal with knife, fork and glass. We must do it again.

A suitable occasion suddenly occurs to me. I shall be going to Burgundy in November to take a look at the Beaune wine auctions, and to attend the wine-growers' lunch at the Chateau de Meursault. Perhaps, I say to Sadler, if he is free, he'd like to come and hold my coat. I can tell the idea interests him.

'A serious lunch, is it?'

'The lunch to end all lunches,' I tell him. 'A good five hours.'

'The finest of wines, no doubt?'

'The very finest. Dozens of them.'

'Done,' says Sadler. 'I'll wear my medal.'

It is rare for me to return home after one of these celebrations without a few accidental souvenirs decorating my clothes. This time, my wife pointed out that in the heat of the moment I seemed to have sat on, or in, some Livarot. My trousers had suffered. In fact, I doubted they would ever recover.

Fortunately, madame who presides over the dry cleaner's shop in Apt is a true artist. Wine, sauce, gravy, oil, butter – none of these has ever resisted her attentions. But even she was impressed by the smears of well-entrenched cheese. Too polite to inquire exactly how they had come to be there, she asked instead what kind of cheese it was. When told it was Livarot, she nodded thoughtfully and offered to clean the trousers for nothing. It was a challenge to her professionalism, she said. Moral: only sit on the very best cheeses.

8

A connoisseur's marathon

THE COURSE CONFORMS precisely to the official distance: 26 miles, 385 yards, or 42.195 kilometres. And there, any resemblance to a conventional marathon ends.

Runners are encouraged to wear fancy dress, the fancier the better. To refresh them during their exertions, wine of very superior quality is available at twenty different *points de dégustation* along the course. It is unlikely that those who stop for a quick one will shatter any world records, but in this convivial race, speed is far less important than enjoyment. A

good time – a memorable time – will be had by all, because
the competitors are taking part in France's most civilized contribution to the sport of long-distance running, one that takes
place in some of the most civilized countryside on earth. This
is the Marathon du Médoc, run through the great vineyards of
Bordeaux.

I have never associated running with fun, and certainly
never with alcohol. The earnest joggers that one sees shuf-
fling through their paces on city streets or along country lanes
show all the signs of joy you would expect to find in torture
victims – eyes glassy, mouths gaping, faces clenched, sweat
and suffering oozing from every pore. Their minds are
undoubtedly more concerned with chipped metatarsals and
the horrors of chafed nipples than with the pleasures of a
glass of wine. To me, running has always looked like a joyless
and painful business, a hobby for masochists.

When I heard about the Marathon du Médoc, the thought
of meeting a different kind of runner – one with a fondness
for dressing up and a taste for the grape – was much too
interesting to miss. Here was an opportunity to fill one of the
many gaps in my sporting education. There were also, I
admit, a couple of ulterior motives: I'd never seen the
chateaux of Bordeaux, some of the most elegant country
houses ever built. And then there were the liquid inducements: Lynch-Bages, Lafite-Rothschild, Phélan Segur, Latour,
Pontet-Canet, Beychevelle, Cos d'Estournel – if there were to
be a wine list in heaven, selected by the Great Sommelier in
the sky, these names would belong in it.

While practising with my corkscrew one evening, I

thought about other trips I'd taken to attend events in unfamiliar parts of France, and how often they had been exercises
in blind optimism. There is a date, and there are a few sketchy
programme details provided by a volunteer organizer – the
mayor's wife, the captain of the fire brigade, the local
butcher – but that's all. You have no idea, until you get there,
whether you're going to find a festive crowd filling the streets
or three men and a morose dog sitting by themselves in the
village square.

This was in a different league altogether. Faxes flew; information arrived. Nothing was too much trouble for the
marvellous Madame Holley, who works for the regional
tourist board. And then one morning, a fax arrived that made
my wife suddenly realize there might be more to running
than she had thought. If I had no other plans, said the invitation from Madame Holley, perhaps I'd like to stay at the
Chateau Pichon-Longueville.

I could see a gleam in the wifely eye at the idea of a chateau
weekend. 'I don't think I've ever told you,' she said, 'but I've
always wanted to watch a marathon.'

We arrived in the late afternoon, with the September sun
tilting across the vines and bathing the chateau in a flattering
wash of pale gold; not that Pichon-Longueville needs any
flattery. It was built in 1851, a period in architecture when
turrets were all the rage, and Pichon (it's nice to be on first
name terms with a chateau) could be the model for a fairytale
castle, suitable for princesses or damsels in distress. The turrets, sheathed in slate, as black and pointed as witches' hats,
rise at each corner of a steeply pitched roof. The windows are

large and perfectly proportioned, and there is a short, graceful flight of stairs leading up to the main entrance. From
there, you can pretend for a few minutes to be part of the
wine-growing nobility, and, from the eminence of your
chateau, look out at your view.

The garden shows you at a glance how the chateau people
of Bordeaux deal with nature: they discipline it. They
straighten it, they form it, they clip it, they smooth it. Trees
are lined up in avenues as if on parade, or planted in strictly
symmetrical groups. Lawns are shaved, gravel is raked, and
water – in this case, a small lake within a rectangular border
of stone – is contained. Beyond the lake, on the other side of
the road, the horizon is green. Vines, as far as you can see, are
trimmed to exactly the same height.

The only traces of disorder to be seen that afternoon were
human. Trestle tables were being unloaded from caterers'
trucks and set up in front of the lake, with crates of glasses
and bottles being unpacked, polished, and laid out. Six hundred runners were coming to dinner at the chateau, and
aperitifs would be served in the garden. There was no doubt
about it; this was already turning into my kind of marathon.

Leaving the impeccable gardens, we found ourselves waist-
deep in equally impeccable vines. Pichon has about seventy
acres of them, with a rosebush at the end of each row acting
as a decorative health warning system. Bugs and ailments
attack roses before they attack vines, so the *vigneron* has a
chance to see the problem and treat it before any serious
damage is done to the grapes. And there they were, little
jewels, dense purple clusters of Cabernet Sauvignon, hanging

from vines that had been struggling in the dry, sandy soil for thirty or more years. 'Vines must suffer' is a phrase you hear frequently in Bordeaux. And I think there must be a local law against weeds. We looked for one as we walked through the rows of vines. We might as well have been looking for the proverbial needle.

The amount of work, much of it manual, involved in maintaining a great vineyard defies description. The initial investment is colossal. The risks of weather are beyond man's control: too much rain, no rain at all, hailstorms, freak winds, late frosts, early frosts. Everything can be done perfectly for eleven months of the year and destroyed overnight. I can never open a bottle of wine without thinking of the effort and skill and patience that have gone into it, and what a bargain it is.

Thirsty thoughts.

They were interrupted by the sound of a jazz band coming from the direction of the chateau. We walked back to the strains of 'When The Saints Go Marching In,' and as we got closer to the gardens, we could hear the buzz of a crowd. The runners had arrived, and the aperitifs were flowing.

It made an incongruous sight: the chateau and its gardens, splendid in their dignified formality, and the decidedly informal crowd, many of whom were dressed as if the race were just about to start. Double-decker running shoes, short shorts revealing some very serviceable-looking thigh and calf muscles, sleeveless vests, T-shirts, back packs, baseball caps – this was evening dress for some of our dinner companions, who all appeared to be in the best of spirits. And why not? It was a glorious evening, more fine weather was forecast for tomorrow's race – it never rains for the marathon, so we were told – and rumour had it that the dinner would be a runners' special, with *hydrates de carbone* galore.

But first, a drink in the chateau with Sylvie Cazes-Régimbeau, who takes care of public relations for Pichon. Charming, and apparently unflustered despite her six hundred dinner guests, she gave us champagne and some impressive statistics.

From nineteen thousand applicants for this year's race, eight thousand had secured places. Of these, there were six thousand *déguisés* in fancy dress, while the rest were more serious runners, including the current champion of France. The youngest runner this year was twenty; the oldest, seventy-five. More than fifty thousand spectators were expected.

The marathon had been founded sixteen years earlier, and three of the five founders were doctors. Thanks to their influence, the medical support would have done credit to a hospital emergency ward: three hundred volunteers – heart specialists, interns, nurses, and foot doctors; fifteen massage tents; cardio-vascular tests; everything from an ingrowing toenail to an erratic pulse or a heart murmur had been anticipated and prepared for.

And the stomach would also be well served. Apart from the twenty-two stands along the course offering high-energy snacks (and 35,000 litres of Vittel mineral water), the famished runner could choose from 15,000 oysters, 400 kilos of entrecôte steak or 160 kilos of cheese. With appropriate wines, naturally. It almost made me want to take up running.

From the gardens below, we could hear the sound of mass movement, the rumble of a migrating herd. The runners were going to dinner. I looked through the window and saw them making for the starting line, which was the entrance to a vast tent that had been put up behind the chateau.

'*Bon,*' said Sylvie. 'Let's go and eat.'

We walked into a wall of sound, as though the party had been going on for hours, although the runners hadn't even sat down. The *animateur* on the stage was having a hard time getting his audience to keep quiet while he introduced some of the competitors from all over France and from all around the world: Argentinians, Brazilians, Poles, Mexicans, Japanese, Americans, British, Canadians, Danes, a couple from New Caledonia, a single intrepid Israeli. Each introduction nearly brought the tent down with roars of applause.

'Please! Please! *Un peu de calme!*' said the *animateur*, holding up his hand in an attempt to reduce the racket, 'I must ask you all to refrain from standing on the tables, at least until dinner is over.' And I'd always thought of runners as quiet and well-behaved.

The tent, big enough to cover most of the lawn behind the chateau and high enough to accommodate a twenty-foot tree, was pulsing with energy – the collective anticipation of six hundred race-trained, physically fit people absolutely bursting to have a good time. Another roar greeted the arrival on stage of the band's lead guitarist, who, either for athletic or musical reasons, hoisted his instrument high over his head while he tuned up and while we studied the menu.

As promised, it was rich in carbohydrates, but these were carbs *à la bordelaise*, starting with a cold pasta salad with ham, followed by noodles and seafood, before moving on to *macaronis et daube au vin du Médoc* – more pasta, with a thick, alcoholic beef stew. There were mountains of bread, and four different wines; two white, two red. Not being blessed with an athlete's cement-mixer metabolism, I found it impossible to believe that anyone would be able to walk the morning after a dinner like this, let alone run.

And now, with an introduction from the *animateur*, who gratefully exchanges his microphone for a glass of wine, the stage is left to the band. They are *très, très cool*, with dark glasses and black fedoras, and as the first course is served, they plunge straight into the sixties, where they will stay for most of the evening. As the first slow chords of 'Sitting On The Dock Of The Bay' roll through the tent, there is an eruption of whistles and claps and yips from nearby tables, where the runners are showing a marked preference for wine over water. A man in a red Basque beret, glass in hand, stands up to offer vocal encouragement to the band. The tent vibrates.

Conversation at our table is made difficult by the music,

but Sylvie is somehow able to make sense of a call she takes on her cell phone. 'I can get you both on a helicopter tomorrow morning, if you like,' she says. 'You'll be able to see all eight thousand runners at once.' This reminds me that we are sitting with fewer than 10 per cent of the competitors, and makes me think of the extraordinary feats of organization required to put on an event of this size. I am struck dumb with admiration and a mouthful of pasta.

The band switches to a medley of Aretha Franklin classics. 'Respect' comes belting out of the loudspeakers. The four girl singers are firmly settled in the groove, fedoras abandoned, hair swirling, hips jerking, arms swooping forward with each clap, wailing their doo-wops and uh-huhs and oohs behind the lead singer. Aretha would be proud of them. One of the waitresses is overcome by an attack of rhythm and boogies towards the table, a large tureen of pasta balanced precariously on each hand. The runners are up and dancing, and it's anarchy on the grass – the bump, the jump, the grind, the Médoc foxtrot, the marathon shuffle, the cardio-vascular quickstep. The tent seems to be swaying. The tree in the middle is shaking. I never knew that the final preparations for an athletic event could be this much fun.

The preference for Bordeaux over water continues. Wine is delivered to the tables in six-packs: Tourelles de Longueville '94 and Chateau Pichon-Longueville '92. Our man in the red beret takes advantage of a break in the music to get up and give us his version of a traditional Basque song. This sets off a chain reaction of other more or less musical offerings from tables throughout the tent. German drinking anthems compete with old French favourites, Dutch choruses and one or two completely incomprehensible chants. The mixture of wine and carbohydrates is working.

The band returns, this time for what is announced as *un hommage* to Stevie Wonder, and a conga line forms, weaving through the tables, around the tree and past the stage. A woman in a Stetson hat and a maple leaf T-shirt stops in front of our table to catch her breath. 'Wow,' she says, 'it's not like this in Toronto.' I wonder what the original inhabitants of the chateau would have made of it all.

Towards midnight, the music slows down. The band gives us 'Try A Little Tenderness'. Couples cling together as if glued, hot, happy and exhausted. And tomorrow they're going to run twenty-six miles.

Leaving the tent, we took a turn around the chateau. The crunch of gravel beneath our feet, high stone walls glowing under the floodlights, black turrets silhouetted against the night sky, pinpoints of light scattered along the banks of the Gironde in the distance beyond the vines, stars up above. The air was cool and clean and smelled of autumn. It was a pleasure just to be alive.

We woke early the next morning, just after six, to the rumble of engines. It was still dark as I looked out of the window and saw a stream of lights trickling slowly along the road, cars by the hundred, bumper-to-bumper on their way to Pauillac, where the race was scheduled to start in three hours' time. While my wife immersed herself in the delights of our bathroom – a space big enough to hold a party, with steps leading up to a canopied bath – I tried to make sense of the notes I had made the night before. Poor, crumpled, wine-stained scraps they were, as usual. I always find it difficult to make intelligible notes when I'm enjoying myself, possibly because my hand is often holding a glass when it should be holding a pen. The result is a series of manic scribbles that have to be translated in the sober light of morning. If only someone would give me a photographic memory for Christmas.

Other guests at the chateau were already having breakfast when we went downstairs to the dining room. Three of them were going to take part in the race. They wore shorts and the slightly subdued manner of people who were going to half-kill themselves before lunch. Two were old marathon hands, and they talked about the times they hoped to achieve, based on their experience in previous races. The third, a senior officer in the French navy, told us that this was his first and last marathon. He was running for the hell of it. At least the weather seemed to be on their side – high cloud, light breeze, no sun. Unfortunately for them, this was not to last.

At eight o'clock, the procession of cars was still nose-to-tail, as it had been for the past two hours. But it seems that if you come out of a chateau driveway, you're entitled to the traditional privilege of *droit de seigneur*, and the traffic parted in a most obliging (and in France, highly unusual) way to let us squeeze into the line. Onward to Pauillac we went, with vines to either side, past Chateau Fonbadet, Chateau Cordeillan Bages, Chateau Lynch-Bages, Chateau Bellegrave – all in all, what real estate agents would consider a most desirable neighbourhood.

When we reached Pauillac, it looked as though the wardrobe department had been hard at work on a Fellini movie. The town was swarming with freaks – men and women with Day-Glo wigs, taffeta tutus, religious robes, convicts' stripes, false body parts, horns, chains, tattoos, purple legs, red noses, blue faces. There were even one or two dressed in shorts and running vests.

We climbed to the top of the stand overlooking the starting line. Below us, the main street was jammed solid with a kaleidoscope of boisterous and weirdly dressed competitors. A man disguised as a strawberry stood on one leg, doing his stretching exercises while he talked to his friend, a man with the physique of a rugby player squeezed into a nurse's uniform. The *animateur* working the street was interviewing competitors – 'This is the most fun you can have on two legs!' – and reminding runners to inform officials, before setting off, of their preference for *vin rouge* or *vin blanc*.

Glancing behind me, I was treated to a tranquil and picturesque scene. A line of runners, at least a dozen of them, was strung out along the river bank, their backs to the road. Undeterred by the passing crowds, they had chosen to ignore the discreet and very adequate toilet facilities provided, preferring instead an open-air performance. Marathon or no marathon, a true Frenchman will always find time for the pleasures of the *pipi rustique*.

On the dot of 9.30, the runners set off, led by two very serious-looking young men who had shot away from the line like whippets, hotly pursued by a Playboy bunny wearing black stockings, black wig, white ears and heavy five o'clock shadow. As these three disappeared into the distance, the other eight thousand began to jostle past, waving, singing, shouting to friends. One or two were actually trying to run, although this was almost impossible in the mass of humanity that choked the street. Watching the moving panorama from our place in the stand, we were struck by the number of men dressed as women, a fondness for drag we had not normally associated with athletes. Perhaps we had led sheltered lives. The other great favourite among the male runners was the baby outfit, complete with bib and drooping diaper. Women, on the other hand, were mostly dressed as women: princesses, milkmaids, nuns, Viking maidens. An anthropologist would have had a field day.

It was a good ten minutes before the last luridly dressed transvestite turned the corner and aimed the twin cones of his false bosom in the direction of Chateau Lynch-Bages. The experts standing next to us, clearly sporting men judging by their tracksuits and running shoes, lighted up cigarettes and speculated about the winning time. The champion of France was running – in fact, he had been neck and neck with the Playboy bunny at the start – and the informed estimates were that he would be crossing the finish line in well under two and a half hours. It was doubtful whether he'd be stopping for any *dégustations* en route, but at least he'd pick up the winner's prize – not a medal, not a silver cup, not a shield, but something useful: his weight in wine.

The less athletically committed spectators began to drift off to spend the morning exercising their arms in the town's bars and cafés until the return of the front runners. We bundled into our car and headed for our first stop, Chateau Pontet Canet.

Grape-growing country starts just outside Pauillac, and the land is clearly too precious to waste on wide roads. These were little more than tracks, narrow, unmarked and hemmed in by vines that grew almost up to the edge of the tarmac on either side. We were driving through green tubes – identical green tubes of identical height and texture. There were occasional aids to navigation: a massive stone crucifix rising above the sea of vines, a distant turret, a boundary stone. Otherwise, we saw only green, flat green, all the way to the horizon. It helps to be born here if you want to find your way.

Pontet Canet was, as it has been since the eighteenth century, magnificent. Not a blemish in the curved gravel driveway, not a twig out of place in the gardens. As we came up to the courtyard, we could hear above the applause and cheering of the spectators the unexpected wheeze and wail of bagpipes. 'The Runner's Lament', it might have been, or maybe 'Bordeaux the Brave'. I find it difficult to tell with bagpipes. They were being played by a piper in a red beret who was standing with his fellow musicians on an impromptu stage made from wooden wine crates. From his beret, I thought he was Basque; from his pipes, Scottish. It turned out he was a Frenchman from Pauillac.

In front of the bandstand was a wine stand, one of the twenty dotted along the course, and the runners had to pass within six feet of it on their way through the courtyard. Many didn't make it – distracted, possibly, by a man from the chateau team, who had stationed himself by the side of the stand, where he stood like a two-fisted Statue of Liberty, arms upraised, a welcoming glass of Pontet Canet in each hand. The dedicated runners, clutching their flasks of Vittel, turned their faces away from temptation and continued onward. Others pulled up with gusty sighs of relief, armed themselves with glasses, and gathered round the *dégustation* table to compare notes with their fellow athletes.

You might expect them to have discussed times, hamstring cramps, and race tactics, but no; as far as I could make out, it was fashion and beauty all the way. One man was having a problem with his mascara, which had run into smudges over his cheeks so that he resembled a startled raccoon. Another had discovered that his long taffeta skirt had a tendency to stick uncomfortably to his perspiring thighs. A third complained of aching lobes, brought on by the excessive weight of his ornamental earrings. The only cure for these assorted ills was, of course, another glass of Pontet Canet.

Watching the runners come up the driveway, I was struck by the total absence of grim-faced competition. They weren't trying to beat each other, but were encouraging each other, dropping back to keep a straggler company, staying in groups instead of single file. Nowhere could I see any sign of the traditional loneliness of the long-distance runner. It wasn't that kind of race.

Knots of spectators were lining the course – clapping, hooting, whistling, cheering, some with personalized banners saying *Allez, Jean-Luc!* or *Vite, Gerard, Vite!* 'Fatigue is purely mental,' I heard one enthusiast shouting. 'You're not tired. You're just thirsty.' By now, the sun had come out, and it wasn't really the weather to be wearing layers of fancy dress. Marie Antoinette came hobbling up the slope to the chateau, one hand clutching his water bottle, the other holding up the folds of his crinoline. I was beginning to understand why so many men had chosen to run as babies, wearing diapers that left their legs bare.

Another mystifying voyage through the vines brought us to Chateau Lafite-Rothschild, the home of what has been called the most beautiful and aristocratic drink in the world. It is a suitably beautiful and aristocratic setting – the house on top of a small hill overlooking a lawn like a billiard table, a park, a lake with a central fountain, rows of gigantic weeping willows. And, as befits this most eminent of chateaux, a twenty-piece orchestra to greet the runners with some musical encouragement.

Adding an exotic touch to this refined sylvan scene were some of the more picturesque competitors: the seven dwarfs scuttled past (minus Snow White, who was probably detained at a previous tasting), followed by a bumblebee, and a bride in a long dress, sunglasses and luxuriant moustache. And there, pausing by the *dégustation* table, was a gentleman dressed as . . . what, exactly?

On his head was an iridescent, emerald green shoulder-length wig. Slung around his neck was a harness in the shape of two monumental corset-pink breasts that bounced against his chest. An apron covered the rest of the frontal scenery as far as the knee, but this token gesture of modesty was rather spoiled when he turned around. On his naked back had been painted an arrow that pointed to his equally naked bottom, which had been attractively priced in bold numerals at 400 francs.

There he stood, in these incomparably distinguished surroundings, enjoying a musical interlude, sipping his glass of Lafite-Rothschild, at peace with the world. He had run twenty-five kilometres and looked set for another twenty, providing his apron stayed put.

A few minutes later, we were getting another view of Chateau Lafite, this time from five hundred feet up. I have mixed feelings about flying in a helicopter. I'm not sure I like the idea of being an aerial Peeping Tom, poking my nose into what is normally hidden behind walls and hedges. It is undoubtedly an invasion of privacy, and therefore something I tell myself I shouldn't be doing. On the other hand, it's fascinating. And the view on this sunny morning was extraordinary.

It was gardening on the epic scale. Mile after mile of barbered symmetry, the chateaux with their turrets and slate roofs like islands in a perfectly smooth green ocean of vines. Thousands of acres of tamed nature. Is there anywhere else in the world where so much land has been so meticulously and elegantly maintained?

The sandy roads cutting through the vineyards were teeming with a long, long line of brightly coloured insects – the runners, by now stretched over several miles. From our seat in the sky they seemed barely to be moving. It was as though someone had sprinkled confetti over the landscape.

With a final swoop across the Gironde, the helicopter set us down behind the stand. It was now 1.30, four hours after the start of the race, and a steady stream of runners was sprinting, jogging, or tottering up the red carpet that led to the finish line, the nirvana of the massage tables, and some restorative carbohydrates provided by a team of caterers called the *Joyeux Tartineurs*.

We sat down for lunch in the stand, and for once the distractions of the view took precedence over the food. There was Yasser Arafat puffing up to the finish, closely followed by a man wearing false buttocks and what looked like an orange tea-cosy. Cleopatra came next, his wig askew, then a man who miraculously still had enough wind left in him to be talking on a cell phone.

The clock above the finish line showed that four and a half hours had elapsed since the start of the race, and still they came: Mickey Mouse, a team of devils in black cloaks and wilted red horns waving tridents, five stout babies running hand in hand, a trio of Scotsmen in tam-o'-shanters and vestigial kilts, a gendarme handcuffed to his prisoner, doctors pushing a stretcher with a very lively patient waving to the crowd and, amid great cheers, a giant bottle of wine with legs. *Vive le Médoc!*

Behind the finish line, we picked our way through a morass

of bodies in various stages of recovery. Some were flat out on the grass, others slumped on the pavement or draped across trestle tables, expressions of bliss on their faces as their muscles melted under massage. A little further along the road, the cafés were filled with nuns and cavemen and hirsute cherubs refuelling. *Pommes frites*, beer, baguettes, cheese, sausage – anything to feed the post-marathon famine – were disappearing as fast as the waiters could bring them out. And these were just snacks. Later, there would be another onslaught of pasta for dinner.

Five hours since the start, and still they came: a sprightly dog towing his owner up to the finish on the end of a leash, a British policeman, Bacchus, a waiter in a top hat, Adam and Eve. We heard that the champion of France had come in first, with a time of two hours and twenty minutes, but this was very clearly not a race of winner and losers. It was a celebration.

We had dinner that night with two of the runners, Pierre and Gerard. One had come from Lyon, the other from Washington D.C., and they had competed in many marathons before. This one, they agreed, was special in many ways. The organization had been faultless, from the pre-race carbohydrate binge to the post-race massage. The good humour, the tremendous sense of comradeship and enjoyment during the race, the costumes, the weather, the beauty of the course – they had all contributed to a rare and remarkable day.

Gerard held up his glass, which was filled with Chateau Lynch-Bages 1985. '*En plus*,' he said, 'the refreshments are particularly agreeable.'

9

Among flying corks in Burgundy

'WHATEVER ELSE YOU do,' I said to Sadler, 'remember to spit. Otherwise, we'll never get through the weekend.'

'I'll watch you,' he said. 'We'll spit together, like they do in synchronized swimming.'

We were in Burgundy, with our wives to keep an eye on us, to attend the greatest wine auction in the world, held each year in Beaune. I had been once before, with another friend who was a Chevalier du Tastevin, a knight of the grape, and the experience had taught me what had to be done if you wanted to survive: spit. Spattered trousers and purple shoes are a small price to pay for the continued health of your internal organs, your ability to focus and to speak, and your reputation as a civilized man able to hold his alcohol.

The sadness is, as I told Sadler, that you will often be spitting when every taste bud in your palate is begging you to swallow, because in Beaune, during this one long weekend, you will be offered dozens, if not hundreds, of some of the finest wines in France. Those names that you gaze at wistfully on restaurant wine lists – those three-hundred-dollar bottles of Burgundian nectar – are uncorked and passed around with the generous abandon normally associated with lemonade on a hot day. But spit you must. There are three days of this to get through, and you'll never be there at the finish if you swallow everything that's waved under your nose.

The tradition started, oddly enough, with a hospital. In 1443, Nicolas Rolin, chancellor to Duke Philip the Good of Burgundy, founded the Hospices de Beaune and endowed the foundation with vineyards to provide it with income. Other charitable Burgundians followed his example, and today, more than five hundred years later, the hospital costs are still covered by revenue from the wine. Every year, traditionally on the third Sunday in November, the wine is sold at auction. And every year, on the days before and after the auction, the local winegrowers arrange a few diversions of their own.

We were invited to one of them on our first night in Burgundy, a *diner dégustation* at the home of René Jacqueson, a grower in Gevrey-Chambertin. It was to be a gentle introduction to the bottles that lay ahead, and it began in Monsieur Jacqueson's private *cave*.

Down a steep flight of steps we went, inhaling the subter-
ranean bouquet, a wonderful musty mixture of oak, wine,
ancient cobwebs, and chilled stone. The *cave* wasn't large – by
Burgundian standards, at least – but it had been beautifully
furnished with several thousand gallons of Gevrey-
Chambertin, stored in barrels that lined walls furred and
blackened with cellar mould. On top of another barrel in the
middle of the room were glasses and half a dozen bottles,
each identified by the wine-maker's shorthand of chalk squig-
gles. But I saw nothing in the way of spitters' comforts.

'There's no bucket,' I whispered to Sadler. 'I think it would
be rude to spit on the floor. We'll have to swallow.'

He took the news bravely. 'Just this once,' he said.

There were two other couples with us, and we gathered

around Jacqueson as he uncorked the first bottle and started
to take us through the vintages. At most other tastings I've
attended, this is as close to a religious ceremony as you can
get without actually going to church. The wine's age and
pedigree are announced in the manner of a bishop murmur-
ing a benediction. The assembled congregation sniffs and
gargles with furrowed brow. Then it's time for prayers, in the
form of solemn, muted comments about the wine's quality:

'Exceptionally self-assured . . . Marvellous finish . . . Classically structured . . . Amen.'

Jacqueson, however, was not at all of the reverent school of wine-makers. He was a man with a twinkle in his eye and a great sense of humour, particularly when he started talking about the overblown language often used on these occasions.

'This one, for instance,' he said, holding his glass up to the light, 'is what you and I might simply call a promising young wine.'

We all sipped and gurgled. At this early stage in its development, there was enough tannin in it to pucker the liver, although it would probably be wonderful when it grew up.

Jacqueson grinned. 'An expert has described it as "having the impatience of youth," whatever that means.'

This led to another old classic: 'Isn't this wine a little young to be up so late?' And as more bottles were uncorked and more barrels tapped, we compared wine-tasting phrases that were unusual or grotesque enough to stick in the mind. Some, like *le goût de la planche*, were logical and accurate. New wine in oak barrels will often have the woody taste of a plank. Other terms were nothing more than desperately far-fetched and unappetizing comparisons: wet leather, wet dogs, weasels – and, my favourite candidate from the animal kingdom, a hare's belly. I have never come across anybody who has admitted to being on tasting terms with a hare's belly – or a weasel or a wet dog, for that matter – and quite how these creatures have crept into the wine taster's vocabulary is something of a mystery. I suppose the problem is that normal descriptions, those words like fruity, powerful, well-made or complex, are too general. They apply to too many wines. And so the weasels and the hares' bellies are brought out in an attempt to express the differences between one wine and another.

This brought the conversation around to professional wine critics, those poor souls who have to strain their imagination and syntax every day in the course of their work, trying to describe what is often indescribable. The prize for the most outlandish description of the evening went to this exchange, reportedly true, between a critic and a grower.

Critic (having swilled, sluiced, and spat): 'Hmm. A distinct *goût de tapis*.'

Grower (outraged): 'What do you mean, a taste of carpet? How dare you!'

Critic (trying to make amends): 'But no ordinary carpet, my friend; a very old, very *distinguished* carpet.'

Our host was far too discreet to name the critic. All he would say was, 'We would prefer him to do his drinking in Bordeaux.'

And with that, we went upstairs to dinner.

It was a marvellous marathon of a meal, five courses prepared by Madame Jacqueson, with a selection of Gevrey-Chambertins prepared by her husband. And in the intermission between the duck and the cheese, there was a music lesson.

It was absolutely necessary, so Jacqueson informed us, that we learn the ritual gestures and lyrics of the 'Ban de Bourgogne'. This was the Burgundian battle cry, a chant accompanied by rhythmic clapping and arcane signals, a kind of drinker's hand jive. We were told it would be performed many times over the weekend, and if we wanted to be part of the festivities, we had to know how to join in.

The lyrics of the chant were no problem: 'La La La La' just about covered them, sung or shouted, according to choice, from beginning to end. The hand movements were slightly more complicated. Starting position was with arms bent and the hands, with fingers cupped, held up on either side of the head. With the first chorus of La La's, the hands should swivel back and forth from the wrist, as if rotating some circular object, such as the base of a wine bottle. For the middle chorus, the hands should stop swivelling to clap nine times before returning to their original positions for the third chorus. This was to be repeated a second time, at top speed, before participants were allowed to recover with the help of a glass of Gevrey-Chambertin.

We tried it. Sadler showed himself to be a natural, with a wonderfully fluid wrist action and a fine profundo bawl. The rest of us did as best we could, making the house sound as though it had been invaded by a bunch of well-oiled football fans. More rehearsals had us bellowing and swivelling our hands like native-born Burgundians, and by the time we left the Jacquesons around one o'clock in the morning, we were judged to be competent enough to perform in public.

As we walked back through the narrow streets, Sadler and I compared spitting notes, and we had to agree that the evening had been a pathetic failure. Number of wines tasted: approximately twelve. Number of times wine ejected from mouth before swallowing: nil.

'We have to do better tomorrow,' I said. 'Expectorate or perish.'

'The problem is,' he said, 'that we need something to do it in. A *crachoir*. Maybe we should buy a bucket.'

The next morning found us window-shopping for portable spittoons in Beaune, a handsome, dignified town that has clearly enjoyed hundreds of years of prosperity. The buildings are stone-built, thick-walled, often with steeply pitched roofs decorated with polychrome tiles. There are cobbled streets and courtyards, ramparts and Gothic architectural flourishes and, wherever you look, evidence of what makes the whole place tick.

Wine. Bottles of it, barrels of it, *caves* to taste it in, thermometers to check its temperature, glasses of every shape and size, corkscrews ranging from the standard waiter's friend to elaborately engineered gadgets for the mechanically minded, silver tasting cups, keyrings disguised as bunches of grapes, decanters, pipettes, and enough alcoholic literature to start a boozer's library. I imagine you could buy a box of Kleenex somewhere in town, but the chances are it would have a vintage chart printed on it. Local industry is keenly supported everywhere you look, with one notable exception: an official Burgundian *crachoir* doesn't seem to exist. I had been hoping to equip myself with something functional yet elegant, perhaps engraved with the Beaune coat-of-arms, or an encouraging motto, or the mayor's autograph, but all we could find were inducements to swallow rather than spit. To his credit, Sadler bore this disappointment well.

Even the medical community in Beaune encourages something a little stronger than aspirin and Alka-Seltzer to relieve what ails you. We stopped at a pharmacy near the main square and looked in disbelief at the contents of the window. Normally, French pharmacies go in for tasteful displays of truncated plastic torsos wearing trusses, or photographs of perfectly formed young women toying with anti-cellulite devices, but not here.

In the centre of the window was a life-size human skeleton, made from cardboard. A sign beside the grinning mouth of the skull read WITH MODERATION, but this was emphatically contradicted (for medical reasons, I assumed) by the rest of the display, which consisted entirely of bottles of wine captioned with their amazing restorative properties. If the pharmacist – a man after my own heart – was to be trusted, almost every common ailment could be cured by the appropriate wine.

A twinge of arthritis? Drink rosé. Diabetes or gallstones? Wash them away with a bottle or two of Sancerre. Moulin-a-Vent would take care of your bronchitis, Krug champagne would ward off the flu, and anyone with tuberculosis or polio would benefit enormously from a bottle of Mercurey. Tension would vanish with Pouilly-Fuissé, and, for weight-watchers, daily doses of Côte de Beaune would make 'daily slimming certain'. Other afflictions were mentioned, some of an intensely personal nature, and for everything there was an alcoholic remedy. One exception: due either to oversight or tact, there was no mention of cirrhosis of the liver.

There was just enough time before the first tasting of the day to see what was going on in the stands and bars around the Place Carnot. It was barely 10.30 a.m., but enthusiasts were already taking a pre-lunch snack of oysters and chilled *Aligoté*. A group of Japanese, who obviously never left home without their personal chopsticks, were having some difficulties extracting their oysters, watched with interest by a young man wearing a helium balloon attached to the zipper on his fly. And then, with thunderous drumrolls and piercing whistles, a procession of stilt-walkers took over the square. The sound was enough to cause a sharp pain in the temples, and we were happy to escape to the peace and quiet of a tasting in the *caves* of Bouchard Ainé & Fils.

The Bouchard people have been growing and selling wine since 1750, and as you tour their cellars you cannot help thinking that this may be the perfect spot to sit out a nuclear war or a presidential election. A million bottles, stored in racks and then in endless avenues of barrels, stretched out and disappeared into the gloom. Famous vineyards, great vintages, the scent of wine dozing towards maturity – the hand felt incomplete, indeed naked, without a glass.

Our host took pity on us and led us upstairs to the tasting room, where bottles and glasses were laid out next to plates of *gougères*. These are small, light, delicious nuggets of cheese-flavoured puff pastry that have the effect of softening and thus improving the taste of young wine in the mouth. They are also salty enough to encourage a healthy thirst. But this was to be an exercise in connoisseurship, not an occasion for guzzling. We were shown the stone sinks against the wall and reminded that spitting was recommended for anyone who, like us, had plans to attend the auction that afternoon.

It was interesting to see how a minor sartorial touch separated the practiced connoisseurs from the rest of us. Veteran tasters wore bow ties, or tucked their ties inside their shirts. The wisdom of this became apparent as the first salvo of spitting took place over the sink and the dangling end of the silk tie belonging to a natty gentleman spitting next to me received a direct hit from a shower of Pinot Noir.

'Young wines to begin with,' our host had said. 'Fish before caviar.' And so we started in 1998 and worked our way backward, fortified by *gougères* and, as far as I was concerned, finding it increasingly unreasonable to spit. Young wines were no problem. The test came when age had smoothed out the rough edges and the wine filled the mouth with a soft glow. Others may have found it possible to consign a big, round, luscious 1988 Fixin to the sink without a sense of loss, but not me. To distract myself, I studied the techniques of other tasters, and they put my simple sniffing and swilling to shame.

In contrast to the informal tasting of the night before, this was a serious ritual, conducted with immense deliberation.

First, the wine is held up to the light, in this case one of the candles in the tasting room, to assess its colour. It is then swirled around the glass to open it up to the air and bring out the bouquet. The nose is applied to the top of the glass for several rapt moments, with the obligatory furrowed brow. A mouthful is taken, the eyes are raised to heaven, and the sound effects begin. Air is sucked into the mouth to join the wine, making much the same noise as a child eating soup. The wine is distributed throughout the mouth, assisted by flexing of the cheeks and exaggerated chewing motions. More gurgling. Finally, when a thorough oral investigation has taken place – the teeth having been rinsed, and the palate imbued with taste sensations – out comes the mouthful to splatter against the stone sink, your shoes and your trousers. You can imagine how this routine, repeated twenty or thirty times with breaks for learned discussion about the character of the wines, can easily take up an entire morning.

We left the *cave*, and had to dodge a second squad of stilt-walkers who were tottering down the street. Cars had been banned from the centre of town for the weekend, but there was still a risk of being run over by some of the pedestrians. Many of them were carrying silver *tastevins* and weaving erratically through the crowd with the preoccupied air of people determined not to miss a single tasting. There were several to choose from; a full day's work if you were up to it and didn't have a busy afternoon ahead.

Over lunch, we were given a briefing by a young and impressively well-informed lady from the Beaune tourist office. This, she told us, was the oldest charity auction in the world, now in its 140th year. The prices paid for the Hospices wines would be a guide to the prices of Burgundy generally, and historically they went up. And up. And up. In 1990, the average price of a *pièce*, or lot, was 350,000 francs. By 1999, it had risen to 456,000 francs. Total sales in the same period had gone from 21 million francs to 31 million. Add to that the cost to the buyer of keeping the wine for several years, bottling, shipping, and a reasonable profit, and it is easy to see why those three-digit prices appear with such horrifying regularity on restaurant lists.

Even so, there was no shortage of buyers, as we saw when we arrived at the auction. The long, high room was filled with them – mostly professional *négociants* from America, Britain, France, Germany, Hong Kong, Japan, Switzerland – all bent diligently over their catalogues. There was also a scattering of black-clad refugees from show business, one or two glamorous women of a certain age who would not have looked out of place at a fashion show as they crossed their legs and adjusted their sunglasses against the glare of publicity, and an assortment of gentlemen from the media, festooned with electronic appendages.

Bidding began just after 2.30 p.m., with bids being picked up by *rabatteurs*, the auctioneer's assistants who were stationed at various points around the floor. Their task wasn't easy. I looked in vain for any exuberant or even obvious signals from the buyers – a hand upraised, a wave of the catalogue, a recurring cough – but there was nothing that demonstrative. It was clear that some very low-key sign language was being used; perhaps no more than the twitch of a pencil or the tap of a nose. It was equally clear that this was not the place to make expansive gestures. One false twitch could cost you dearly, and I noticed that even the French were keeping their hands uncharacteristically still while they muttered among themselves.

As the bidding continued, the smile grew on the auction-eer's face. Once again, prices were up. We learned later that the average increase had been 11 per cent. A good day for charity, a good day for Burgundy, and, of course, a good day for Beaune. Walking back through town after the auction, we passed the pharmacy with the skeleton, and the skull's grin seemed to be even wider, as if reflecting the general mood of satisfaction with another record year.

Our day was far from over. Dinner that night – a gala dinner at the Hôtel-Dieu – promised to be the most formal event of the weekend. *Tenue de soirée*, or evening dress, was to be worn. We were advised to take a large spoonful of olive oil, neat, to line the stomach in preparation for the downpour of wine. This was not to be an evening of spitting. Another essential, so we were told, was a pair of thick socks to ward off the chill from the flagstone floor – a tip that was wasted on our wives, who felt that socks and evening dresses were somehow not what they wanted to be seen in.

We arrived, as requested on the invitation, at 9.00 p.m., making our way through a double line of white-coated wait-ers into a magnificent barrel-vaulted room hung with tapestries. Candlelight flickered on the bottles and glasses and silverware that had been laid out on thirty-one long, immaculately arranged, and surprisingly empty tables. Where was everybody? There was not a sign of our three hundred fellow revellers, and it was then I remembered that punctuality on formal occasions in France is seldom rewarded by a welcoming glass. Politeness dictates that you wait until the other guests have arrived. They, naturally, would prefer to avoid having to endure a long, dry waiting period, and therefore they make a point of always being fashionably late. So there we were, surrounded by glorious but untouchable bottles. 'Meursault, Meursault everywhere,' as Sadler said, 'and not a drop to drink.'

This would pass, we told each other, and picked up the menus in search of a little encouragement. There was a long and heartfelt sigh from Sadler as he reached the page listing the wines that were on offer that evening: thirty-eight of them, the great whites and reds of Burgundy, donated by growers and *négociants*, the Hospices de Beaune and the mayor. Such a list you would find nowhere else, filled with Grand Cru Chablis, Puligny-Montrachet, Echezeaux, Clos Vougeot – the kind of wine Alexandre Dumas said should be drunk kneeling, with the head bared.

It was half an hour before the last empty seats and the first empty glasses were filled. The great room was a picture of elegance: the bejewelled ladies in long dresses (some of them so long I suspected them of concealing thick socks), the gentlemen in their black and white, hair and moustaches sleek with pomade, cuff links and shirt studs twinkling. It was a scene of refined formality. It was destined not to last.

The crack in the social ice came with the appearance, early

on in the dinner, of the cabaret, a male vocal group introduced as Les Joyeux Bourguignons. They were dressed in
their best long aprons, red and green pompoms at their necks
in place of ties, glasses and bottles in their hands instead of
musical instruments. They set the tone for the rest of the
evening with their first song, a perennial local hit entitled
'*Boire un petit coup c'est agréable*' (rough translation: 'It's great
to drink'). This was followed by an audience participation
session as we were led into the first of many renditions of the
Burgundy supporters' club battle cry. La La's were bellowed
and hands were waggled. Almost at once, formality disappeared, never to return.

The food came and went, the bottles came and came, and
inhibitions began to be cast aside like corks. A group at a
nearby table stood up to perform a series of Mexican waves
with their napkins, while one of the men – intent on
striptease, by the look of him – climbed up on his chair and
ripped off his jacket and tie before being distracted and ulti-
mately subdued with the help of a bottle of Aloxe-Corton.
Toasts were proposed: to the greater glory of the grape, to the
continuing success of the Channel Tunnel, to the *entente cor-
diale*, to heroes of the Swiss Navy, to anything else that might
provide an excuse for glasses to be refilled. Not that excuses
seemed to be necessary.

I looked down the table at Sadler, who was investigating a
bottle of 1993 Echezeaux. We had often talked about the
enormous difference between popular foreign perceptions of
the French and our own experience of living among them,
and an evening like this emphasized the difference. Where

was he, the so-called typical Frenchman, with his humourless reserve and his arrogance and his infuriating superiority complex? He was certainly not here, not in this warm, friendly, relaxed, and, it must be said, increasingly tipsy gathering. It seemed to me, as the Echezeaux took hold and I looked around, that they were all wonderful people, drinking wonderful wine and living in a wonderful country.

Fixing Sadler with a moist and sentimental eye, I was about to propose a toast to *La Belle France*. How lucky we were to live here, to be surrounded by such delightful people, such splendid architecture, such rich culture, such stirring history, such ravishing countryside. In my wine-sodden French, it would probably have been a disastrously embarrassing moment. Fortunately, Sadler beat me to it.

He raised his glass. I waited for some graceful and appropriate line from Molière or Voltaire or Proust, delivered in perfect, accentless Sadler French. But it was not to be.

'To those who spit,' he said. 'Poor sods.'

It is well known that the better the wine you drink, the less you suffer the following morning, which was just as well. Our previous encounters during Saturday and Sunday – the various tastings and two memorable dinners were, in a way, just a prelude to the climax of this long weekend, the sixty-eighth Paulée de Meursault, a wine-growers' lunch attended by the most distinguished local *vignerons* and their guests. It had started as a small local affair to celebrate a successful *vendange* – so small that it used to be held in the village hall. But Burgundians are hospitable people. The guest list doubled, and doubled again. Eventually, lunch outgrew the hall and had to be moved to the spacious sixteenth-century grandeur of the Chateau de Meursault. This year there would be six hundred of us, and printed on the invitations was a reminder: According to tradition, each brings his own bottles.

Waiting at the entrance to the chateau were half a dozen of Beaune's finest, the local gendarmes. One of them told us where to park the car – 'And don't forget where you've put it,' he said, looking at the bottles in the back. We told him we were going to be picked up by our wives at the end of lunch. 'Of course,' he said, with a noticeable lack of conviction. He saluted and wished us *bon appétit*.

The estates of the Chateau de Meursault, which extend to more than 110 acres, produce seven Grands Crus, and there is never any danger of running short. The chateau *caves* normally contain between 400,000 and 500,000 bottles, and many of the guests – growers, by the look of their wind-blasted complexions and leathery, muscular hands – were arriving not with mere armfuls of bottles, but with crates. Sadler and I joined the crush and filed through to the dining hall, an immense cavern lined with barrels big enough to swim in. Signs hung down from the ceiling over the long tables, an illustrious parade of Meursault vineyards: Les Perrières, Les Charmes, La Pièce-sous-le-Bois, Les Genevrières, La Goutte d'Or. The sound level was already high. These are men who normally hold their conversations in the open, across the width of a field, over the noise of a tractor engine, and they sometimes forget to adjust their volume when they come indoors. Even so, it was possible to hear Burgundy's favourite background music, the steady clink of glass against glass and the irregular fusillade of corks coming out of bottles.

We found our places and took a look at the menu. One of the growers had told us that it would be a modest meal, such as a man might eat after his work in the vines. Judge for yourself. To begin with, there was a terrine of monkfish in bouillabaisse jelly; followed by slivers of fried sole with crayfish dumplings; followed by leg of wild duck, braised in white wine, with stuffed cabbage; followed by filet of venison with redcurrants and quince; followed by a selection of cheeses; followed by a selection of desserts. And then there were the wines.

A hand holding a bottle came over my shoulder and a voice murmured 'Batard-Montrachet '89.' The growers were beginning to circulate, distributing refreshment to everyone within pouring range, and I thought that if wines like this were being thrust upon me, the least I could do was to take notes. That first wine was superb – flowery, soft and dry – and I couldn't imagine taking just one mouthful before tipping the rest into one of the ice buckets provided for dregs. I was a fool, needless to say, but it was still early.

There were musical interludes between each course, provided by our old partners in revelry, Les Joyeux Bourguignons, who were in remarkably good voice for men who had been singing and drinking for several hours the night before. These useful pauses between eating allowed the growers to keep circulating and pouring, and if my notes are anything to go by, we tasted an average of eight to ten wines per course. It was a slow and delicious business, and two hours into the lunch we still hadn't reached the venison. But we had at least arrived at the point where whites were being replaced by reds, and it seemed a suitable moment to review the score.

My stained scraps of paper, covered in a visibly degenerating scrawl – I can't keep calling them notes – listed twenty-seven white wines. Some notations were underlined, others marked with appreciative exclamation points or asterisks, but I have to admit that as a detailed and informative record it was a disaster. I can definitely say, however, that neither Sadler nor I sent anything back.

We rather lost track of the reds, but I noticed that a neighbouring *chevalier*, showing superhuman professionalism, was continuing to take notes. He reached a grand total of fifty-nine wines before his aim faltered and he started writing on the tablecloth and giggling.

Coffee came at 6.30, and we sat back and enjoyed the view. The tables around us had turned into bottlescapes. Never had I seen so many opened bottles in a single room, thousands of them, many still half-full, a fortune in leftovers. I longed for a doggy barrel. One of the growers passed us a bottle of his 1991 Corton and invited us to his *cave* for a tasting that evening. He wasn't joking, either.

Memory fails me somewhat after that, although I vaguely remember making plans to go to the pharmacy in the morning for aspirin before seeking out a medicinal bottle of champagne. When we finally left the hall and emerged into the cold November night, we found ourselves in a crowd outside the entrance, listening to an exchange between a gendarme and a gentleman who was complaining that he had mislaid his car. Given the car-owner's condition, I thought he had perhaps chosen the wrong person to complain to. But there was no hint of official censure in the gendarme's voice.

'*Oui, monsieur,*' he was saying with as much patience as he could muster, 'you have told me that your Renault is eluding you. But as you can see, there are many Renaults here. A clue would be helpful. Do you have any recollection of the colour?'

Our car found us, and we settled in; replete, drowsy, and profoundly grateful that we didn't have to drive ourselves back to Beaune. 'That,' said Sadler, 'was a hell of a way to spend Monday.'

10

Aristocrats with blue feet

OVER RECENT YEARS, we have become more and more curious about what exactly it is we put into our stomachs every day – where it comes from, what it contains, what it does to us. We are hungry for information, and the response from those who supply our food and drink has been voluminous. They have swamped us with nutritional facts and analyses, guarantees of goodness, testimonials from dieticians, proof of genuine identity: these assurances are attached to almost everything edible, from those indigestible little stickers on apples and pears to the longer and more learned texts on the back of cereal boxes.

Some of these illuminating notes, however, do nothing to allay the innocent customer's fears and suspicions. Wine, for instance, which we've learned should not be consumed by pregnant women operating heavy machinery, has now owned up to another dark secret, at least in America. Almost every bottle, we are informed by a label on its back, contains sulphites.

Sulphites, according to my dictionary, are salts or esters of sulphurous acid, and they can lead to severe allergic reactions in susceptible individuals. Their use as preservatives of fruit and vegetables was banned by the United States Food and Drug Administration in 1986. And yet there they are, those sulphites, brazen as can be, bobbing around in your Chardonnay. A sobering thought indeed, and one that caused me to make a few apprehensive inquiries. It seems that I needn't have worried; all is well for the vast majority of wine drinkers. The exceptions are usually asthma sufferers – but only very few of them – who might find themselves allergic to sulphites. For the rest of us, a glass or two a day will do more good than harm.

Very little is allowed to escape the current passion for disclosure, and we cannot be far from the day when restaurants will follow the trend to come clean and provide us with more complete information about their specials of the day. Menu writers, of course, will be obliged to extend and amplify their seductive vocabularies: prime aged steak, enhanced with free-range hormones; French beans and garden peas, genetically modified in God's clean fresh air; roast leg of lamb, cloned with loving care; veal chops, with that tasty hint of steroids. And all of it will be prepared by the most sanitary of chefs, wearing rubber gloves and a surgical face mask. No wonder we're growing taller and living longer.

Interest in food and concern about its life before reaching the table are also beginning to have increasing influence over our social behaviour. I read some time ago that a celebratory evening of foie gras at the Smithsonian Institution had to be cancelled because of protests about the way in which the livers of ducks and geese are fattened. This led me to think about another bird, eaten by millions every day, but reared for the most part in conditions of carefully maintained obscurity: the chicken.

In many countries, chicken is no more than a commodity with an enviable reputation – bland, versatile, easy to pre-pare, acceptable to even the most delicate of palates; invalids' food, as harmless as a vegetable, a healthy alternative to heavy red meat. I wonder how long that enviable reputation would survive if more of us were familiar with the methods used to raise some of these unfortunate creatures. Here is a brief extract from an article written by André Giovanni, edi-torial director of *Santé*, a French magazine devoted to questions of health. While it is true that the French pay closer attention to the origins of what they eat than many other nationalities, it's easy to understand Giovanni's distaste and alarm when he describes the typical life cycle of mass-produced chickens:

Squeezed into batteries, fed on products containing
polluted animal matter, stuffed with antibiotics, their
beaks cut off, living their entire lives without seeing
daylight.

And then they're slaughtered and passed along to us. Under
these barbaric but cost-effective conditions, one man can
oversee the rearing of 280,000 chickens a year (compared
with a mere 25,000 a year if more humane methods are used).

No doubt this horrific regime exists in France, as in the rest
of the civilized world. But in France (and, I hope, elsewhere),
there is a choice – or rather a range of choices – that provide
a better life for the chicken, and a better chicken for the consumer. You might call it a pecking order.

At the bottom is the plain old farmyard chicken, raised – *en
liberté*, as the French say – in the open air in the traditional
way, allowed to feed on whatever nature provides. Then we
have the biological or organic chicken, with a controlled diet
that is guaranteed to be free of chemical seasonings. And
finally, there is the ultimate chicken, the only chicken to have
its own *Appellation Contrôlée*, the chicken from Bresse.

I had endured several lectures about the glories of the
Bresse chicken from my friend Régis, who for some years
now has been instructing me as to what I should and shouldn't
eat and drink. But his eulogies, or what I could make sense of
when he wasn't busy kissing his fingertips and moaning with
remembered pleasure while describing some past feast, were
confined to taste and recipes. He was vague on detail, as to
why the flavour was so elegant, so delicate, so exquisite, so

typically *French* (his words, not mine). And so when I heard that the most important event of the chicken year was taking place just before Christmas, I persuaded him to go with me to the town of Bourg-en-Bresse for the annual celebration known as *Les Glorieuses*.

The elite chicken zone of Bresse, about eighty kilometres north of Lyon, forms a rectangle roughly one hundred kilometres long and forty wide. To the west, just the other side of the autoroute, are the illustrious names and vineyards of Burgundy, and as we started seeing road signs to Fleurie and Juliénas and Macon, Régis began to fidget.

'It so happens,' he said, 'that I know a couple of wonderful addresses we could try, not far from here.' He tapped his fingers on the car's dashboard and began to hum in his rather pleasant light baritone as he waited for me to reply.

I had heard that hum before from Régis. I don't think he even knows he's doing it, but it comes out every time he looks at a menu or a wine list. There is clearly a direct line between his vocal chords and his stomach, and the hum is like a radar beep, a signal that something delicious cannot be too far away.

My watch showed 10.30. 'A bit early for lunch, isn't it?'

He turned an innocent face towards me. 'Wine, *mon vieux*, wine. We could slip over to Chiroubles and fill up the car with Beaujolais. A detour, nothing more.' He thought for a moment. 'Although there is the Auberge at Fleurie if we should find ourselves nearby at lunchtime.' He glanced at the map lying open on his lap, and pretended to be surprised. 'Which we would. What a piece of luck.'

'Well, perhaps we could stop on the way back. I don't want to miss the chickens.'

Régis emitted a gusty sigh (and I'd heard plenty of those before, too). 'The trouble with you English,' he said, 'is your reluctance to enjoy yourselves, your distrust of pleasure. What could be more agreeable than a *dégustation* followed by a little light lunch?' The humming resumed.

I ignored his criticism of my fun-loving fellow countrymen. 'Régis, you forget. I know you.'

'So?'

'You haven't had a little light lunch in years. We'd stagger out of the restaurant at three-thirty, looking for somewhere to lie down. This is supposed to be a working trip. We're here to see chickens.'

'*Pouf*,' said Régis, and sulked in silence all the way to Bourg.

The greatest chicken show on earth was taking place at the Parc des Expositions on the outskirts of Bourg-en-Bresse. Here, in a modern complex of enormous exhibition halls surrounded by acres of parking space, you would normally expect to find business conventions of one sort or another, or trade shows promoting the latest in combine-harvester technology. It was a long way from the rolling meadows of the countryside, and seemed an incongruous setting for farmers and poultry.

As we made our way to the information office, Régis was still wearing the doleful air of a man who has been cheated out of his divine right to a long lunch. A brisk, helpful woman brought us up to date on the details of the event. This afternoon, she told us, would be mainly devoted to the opening formalities, with a panel discussion among various movers and shakers from local industries. And in the evening, *bien sûr*, there was the official dinner.

Régis looked sideways at me and then, in a tone of icy politeness, turned to the woman. 'And chickens, madame? When might one expect to see chickens?'

Madame passed him a folder. 'It's all in there,' she said. 'The chickens being exhibited will be arranged in the halls between four-thirty and seven tomorrow morning. The jury convenes at six-thirty and will start judging at seven. Doors will be open to the public at ten. Then, monsieur, you will see your chickens.'

'*Ah bon*,' said Régis, looking at me again. 'Ten o'clock tomorrow morning before we can see any chickens. *Merci*, madame.'

I have spent more convivial afternoons than the one that followed. My companion was a model of reproach, fortunately mostly silent. But he didn't need to speak; the missed lunch – the *needlessly* missed lunch – loomed between us like an unwanted third person. In an effort to distract Régis from thoughts of the flesh I took him to see a local landmark on the outskirts of town, the sixteenth-century church at Brou, a marvel of Gothic architecture, only to find it closed for renovation. It wasn't until we crossed the road to look at the menu posted outside a restaurant, the Auberge Bressane, that a very faint hum hinted at a return to good humour. I thought it was time to make amends.

'I'm sorry about this morning,' I said. 'Bad planning. The least I can do is buy you dinner this evening.'

Régis pretended not to have heard. 'I see they recommend frogs' legs to start with.' The hum returned, a little louder than before. Things were looking up. 'It would be interesting to compare their taste to that of the chicken – one must have chicken when in Bresse, don't you think?' It seemed that all had been forgiven.

We spent what was left of the afternoon exploring Bourg. I was all for buying a chicken to take back to Provence with me, but Régis advised waiting until the next day, when, as we'd been told, there would be no shortage of prime fowl to choose from.

So we went shopping for postcards instead, finding that Bourg-en-Bresse takes its role as chicken capital of the world very seriously. Almost everywhere the tourist sets foot nowadays, from Miami to Monte Carlo, the postcard of choice seems to be a panoramic view of six perfectly formed, perfectly bronzed buttocks belonging to three young ladies clad in G-strings and wishing we were there. I suppose it makes a change from more traditional scenery, but it does little to convey the true spirit of a place (with the possible exception of Miami). In Bourg, however, there is no doubt what the visitor is expected to send home: a poultry card. The favourite is a graphic illustration of three fine and brightly coloured birds – one blue, one white, one red – with a prominent reminder that Bresse chickens are the recipients of an AOC, or *Appellation d'Origine Contrôlée*, a distinction that not even those three well-rounded young ladies could claim.

The honour was officially confirmed in 1957, nearly four hundred years after an entry in the archives of Bresse noted that the local chicken enjoyed a '*belle notoriété*'. This has developed over the centuries into a *renommée mondiale*, a worldwide reputation, and it is a reputation that is jealously protected.

Qualifications are extremely strict. First of all, every chicken worthy of its *appellation* must possess a patriotic external appearance, in colours that happen to repeat the tricolour of the French flag:

• *Blue feet*. But they can't be any old blue; the feet must have the pale gleam of blue steel. And around the left ankle, there must be an aluminium ring marked with the name and address of the farmer responsible for raising that particular chicken.

• *Entirely white plumage*. There can be no hint of the common chicken's dowdy brown tinge.

• *A bright red crest*. In the case of the cockerel, the indentations on the crest must be sufficiently well developed to achieve that desirable look of jagged virility.

In addition to the blue, white and red ensemble, every bird must possess a fine skin, delicate bone structure, and, in the official phrase, unctuous flesh. (I am sure that Bresse is teeming with men who specialize in judging unctuous flesh.) There are even rules about minimum weight: 1.5 kilos (3.3 pounds) for the standard chicken, 2.1 kilos (4.6 pounds) for the *poularde*, or more matronly chicken, and 3.8 kilos (8.4 pounds) for the capon.

These statistics and many others were in the folder that we had picked up at the exhibition hall, and which we were going through over a drink before dinner. I could tell that the information was having an uplifting effect on my friend's disposition. 'You see?' Régis kept saying as he discovered more and more evidence that his beloved France led the world in chicken *de luxe*. 'The care, the attention to detail, the refinement. Is there anything like this in Britain? In America?' He didn't give me a chance to answer. 'Of course not.'

I can imagine that many people might find Régis and his relentless chauvinism a little hard to take, but I like his enthusiasm, biased though it is. I've never met anyone else who combines passion and knowledge – not to mention shameless greed – when it comes to the correct degree of rot in a cheese or the ideal temperature at which to serve tripe. At the same time, his dismissal of what he considers to be inferior food and cooking (that is, almost everything not French) is inventive and often very funny, even if it is highly prejudiced. To hear him denouncing the cheeseburger, or the English way with Brussels sprouts, is to hear a talented gastronomic assassin in full cry. I've often thought he would make a wonderfully savage restaurant critic. That night, however, criticism was far from his mind. His mood had improved to such an extent after two glasses of champagne that it was a distinctly benign Régis who took his place opposite me in the restaurant, humming as he looked around.

The Auberge Bressane sits at the upper end of the scale between the simple bistro and those more elaborate establishments festooned with stars by the Michelin guide. The lighting is soft, the table linen thick, the atmosphere relaxed and comfortable; a man can take off his jacket and tuck his napkin in his shirt collar without fear of provoking a sniff and a raised eyebrow from a sartorially sensitive headwaiter.

After a few minutes of pleasant indecision, we both chose the same dishes: frogs' legs, followed by chicken, with white and red Burgundies from vineyards just the other side of the autoroute. When the bottles were brought to us, I noticed there were no warnings about the presence of sulphites.

'Good God no,' Régis said. 'Not here in France. Not in *Burgundy.* Mind you, one never knows what the law says they have to add when they send it over to America.' He held his glass up to the light and studied the pale golden shimmer of the Meursault. 'Which reminds me . . .'

He chewed on a mouthful of wine before reaching into his pocket. 'I cut this out for you,' he said, smoothing a newspaper clipping on the table in front of him and passing it over to me. 'I thought it was a sign of the times.'

It was an advertisement. A grizzled gentleman dressed as a typical cowboy – work shirt, large hat, picturesque wrinkles – was remarking on the fact that McDonald's, that most American of institutions, was now serving only home-grown French chicken in its restaurants in France. The timing of the advertisement was significant: there had just been a major scandal in neighbouring Belgium involving tainted food, some of it chicken. While across the Channel, the English, perfidious as always, were taking France to court for refusing to accept their beef for fear of *la vache folle*, or mad cow disease. All in all, these were trying times for the country of Brillat-Savarin and Escoffier, and extra vigilance was needed to make sure that unscrupulous foreigners didn't succeed in

foisting suspect food on the trusting French public. The
cowboy was there to reassure McDonald's addicts that correct
Gallic standards were being maintained.

I asked Régis if, in the cause of gastronomic research, he'd
ever been to a McDonald's. He looked at me as though I were
deranged, then shook his head.

'*Moi?*' he said. 'I wouldn't go, as a matter of principle. Do
you know the average time taken to eat a McDonald's meal?
Seven and a half minutes! And they're proud of it! It's an
affront to the digestion. No, you'll never catch me in
McDonald's – although, to be fair, I have heard good reports
about their *pommes frites*.' I saw his nose twitch, and he
turned his head. 'Ah, here come the frogs' legs.'

The essentials were arranged in front of us: two well-filled
plates, still sizzling; finger bowls; a basket of bread. The tiny
aromatic legs had been sautéed with garlic, then dusted with
chopped parsley. After refilling our glasses and warning us
that the plates were hotter than hot, our young waitress
wished us *bon appétit*. Régis bent over to inhale the scent
and, using a piece of bread, manoeuvred his first leg to the
side of the plate, picked it up with careful fingers, and examined it.

'The English don't know what they're missing,' he said,
stripping the flesh off the bone with his teeth. He chewed for
a moment. 'Or are they worried about mad frog disease?' He
dabbed his mouth with his napkin and nodded. 'That must be
it.'

With the assurance that comes from being an official
member of the brotherhood of thigh-tasters of Vittel, I dealt

with my first few legs – moist, almost crisp, with the clean flavour of parsley coming through the garlic. Delicious. Why don't the English eat them? We certainly have the ideal climate for frogs, damp and cool. But then the thought occurred to me that perhaps we have a national aversion to eating things that hop or slither.

'We're not too keen on snails, either,' I said.

'Ah, the snail is different.' Régis sucked a thighbone thoughtfully. 'His purpose in life is to be a vehicle for garlic – good enough, in his way, but he lacks the finesse of the frog.' He wiped his plate with a scrap of bread, rinsed his fingers in the small bowl, and poured more wine. 'Do you think all these people are here for the show?'

I looked around the restaurant to see if I could spot any obvious poultry tycoons, with the odd feather still clinging to their clothes, but it seemed a fairly typical French mixture of friends and families out on a Saturday night. Several children were there, polishing off their grown-up food with adult dexterity, and I was struck, as I often am, by the good behaviour of French children when they are taken to restaurants: no squawks, no tantrums, no ear-splitting demands for three courses of ice cream. And their patience never fails to amaze me. Two hours or more at the table must seem like an eternity to a seven-year-old.

Régis, as usual, had the answer. 'Watered-down wine,' he said, 'that's the secret. It has a very calming effect on the young. Also, it's better for them than any of those gassy sweet drinks. I myself was brought up from the age of six on diluted Côtes du Rhône, and look at me.' He beamed across the table, ruddy-faced and bright-eyed. Heaven knows what his liver looked like, but externally he was the picture of health.

The red wine, a Côte de Beaune from Jadot, was scrutinized, sniffed, rolled around the palate – 'the interrogation of the bottle,' as Régis put it – and pronounced excellent. And then we saw our chicken making its way towards our table, the plates held high by the waitress and protected from the elements by great silver domes, which she removed with a double flourish.

'*Voilà, messieurs – poulet de Bresse à la crème.*' She watched Régis with a smile as he bent over his plate and, with small encouraging flutters of his hand, waved the steam rising from the chicken towards his face. He remained nose down for a moment, inhaling deeply, then nodded two or three times before looking up at the girl.

'Tell me if you would, *mademoiselle*, a little about the recipe.' He wagged an index finger at the waitress. 'No chef's secrets, naturally, just the main ingredients.' Which she did, with the occasional murmured 'Ah yes' or 'Of course' from Régis.

First into the pan goes a generous knob of butter, followed by the chicken breasts and legs, a large onion cut into quarters, a dozen or so sliced *champignons de Paris* – those small, tightly-capped white mushrooms – a couple of cloves of garlic *en chemise*, crushed but not peeled, and a bouquet garni of herbs. When the colour of the chicken has turned to deep gold, a large glass of white wine is poured into the pan and allowed to reduce before half a litre of *crème fraiche* is added. The bird is cooked for thirty minutes, the sauce is strained through a fine sieve, the dish is seasoned to taste, and there you have it. The waitress returned to the kitchen, having made the whole thing sound as easy as preparing a sandwich.

It was a chicken in triumph, we both agreed. Like the frogs' legs, it was moist and tender, almost melting, but with a more defined taste, the flesh as smooth as the cream it had been cooked in. We ate at an old-fashioned, pre-McDonald's pace – slowly, taking pleasure in each mouthful, and in almost total silence. There was nothing to say except God bless the chef.

When our waitress came back, she saw two extremely clean plates. 'So it pleased you, *le poulet?*' Indeed it had, we told her. Unctuous was the only word to describe it. We asked her to present our congratulations to the supplier of the chicken, the chef, and, with our complimentary mood well lubricated by Burgundy, to everyone else who had been involved.

'And how did it compare with the frogs' legs?' she asked. Régis sat back, tapping the fingertips of both hands together while he thought of an appropriate reply. 'Let me put it this way,' he said. 'It was like the difference between a very good wine and one of the great vintages.'

The waitress inclined her head, and shrugged. '*C'est normal*,' she said. 'The chicken, after all, has the *Appellation Contrôlée*. Whereas the frog, no matter how worthy, is still just a frog.' She cleared away our plates and suggested a little local cheese, the Bleu de Bresse, to go with the last of the wine.

The cheese, pungent and creamy enough to coat the palate and flatter the wine, set Régis off on one of the many hobby horses he keeps in his stable: the importance of eating food at the right time of year and in the right place. Strawberries at Christmas, wild boar in June, and all the other exotic delights made permanently available through modern methods of preservation, he rejected with a wave of his glass. That may be fine for supermarkets, he said. But the truly educated gourmet (doubtless a Frenchman) eats only what is in season. And if he's lucky, as we were that night, he eats the local specialties on the spot, where they are produced.

It made excellent sense, I said, as long as our educated gourmet had unlimited time, and the resources to follow his appetite all over the country. As soon as I spoke, I realized I should have known better. Régis leaned forward, his eyes glittering in the candlelight. 'That's it!' he said. 'That's what we should do next – a gastronomic Tour de France. Imagine: those little corners where they produce the best food in the world, and we could be there at the *moment juste* for the asparagus, the spring lamb, the oysters . . .' His face took on the dreamy, faraway expression of a man contemplating an imminent journey to paradise, and it took the offer of a glass of Calvados to bring him down to earth. He was still muttering about larks' tongues and truffles half an hour later, as we walked back to our hotel in the bitter December night air.

The following morning was the moment of truth for the most noble poultry in France. Régis and I were there at the Parc des Expositions as the doors opened, and were swept through in the first wave of enthusiasts. Two vast spaces were devoted to the exhibition, and a quick inspection showed that one was allocated to the living and the other to the dead. Drawn by the sound of chirping, we went first into the hall of the living. In the central space, a series of small fenced gardens had been set up and landscaped with rocks and foliage and verdant artificial grass; lining the outside perimeter of the hall were stalls providing refreshment for those in need.

Régis rubbed his hands as he took stock of the dozens of trestle tables laid out with smoked ham, sausage, cheeses, handmade country bread, pâtés and a selection of wines from as far north as Champagne and as far south as Chateauneuf, the yellow wine of the Jura side by side with Beaujolais and the heavier Burgundies. A greedy and unprincipled man, as Régis observed rather piously, could eat and drink extremely well without spending a centime, simply by taking advantage of the free samples on offer.

I steered him away from a bulging sausage the size of a weightlifter's bicep and over to the heated compound set aside for chicks. Clearly excited by their first public appearance, they were scurrying around and chirping loudly enough to drown the sound of the early morning grumbles of the loud-speaker system. A series of notices planted in the fake grass informed us of the life these chicks could expect. After five weeks in centrally heated *poussiniéres*, they would be let out into the open, with at least ten square metres of grassland per chicken, to spend anything from nine to twenty-three weeks feeding on natural rations (worms, insects, small molluscs), supplemented by maize, wheat and milk. These months in the fields would be followed by a fattening period during which two square meals a day would be served to them in capacious wooden cages. This, apparently, was the secret of the unctuous flesh.

We were able to see the results of this privileged upbringing in a neighbouring compound. It may be difficult to imagine such a thing as a glamorous chicken if you've never seen one, but these were as close as it gets: plumage as white and spotless as fresh snow, vivid red crests, bright and beady eyes, and those aristocratic blue feet. Their walk was stately and deliberate; they paused between steps, holding one foot in the air, as though they were tiptoeing across a sheet of paper-thin ice. Each bird wore the obligatory aluminium ring, stamped with the breeder's name and address, around the left ankle. There is no chance of a Bresse chicken crossing the road and finding anonymity on the other side.

I heard what sounded like a dogfight, followed the noise, and discovered that there was more to the exhibition than chickens. Half a dozen turkeys, magnificent black-feathered beasts a good three feet tall, were complaining – possibly about the uncomfortable proximity of Christmas – their wattles quivering with indignation each time they gave voice. All they needed were pearl necklaces and they could have passed for dowager duchesses bemoaning the declining standards of the House of Lords. They made a curious yapping, not at all the soothing gobble I had expected; more like a squabble of terriers.

Régis had disappeared, and I went to look for him among the crowd. There were farmers and chicken breeders, cheese makers and wine growers, some in suits and ties, their unaccustomed formality sitting uneasily on bodies more used to overalls. There were occasional flashes of chic – women in sleek tweeds and country jewellery, with conspicuously glowing make-up, clean shoes and the odd jaunty hat with a pheasant feather stuck in the band. And then a sight straight out of the nineteenth century, a group of men and women in traditional Bressane costume, waistcoats, breeches, long dresses, bonnets and clogs, clattering off to a corner of the hall.

I tagged along behind them, watching as they adjusted their bonnets and tuned up blunt musical instruments that looked like acoustic tennis rackets. Forming up in pairs, off they went, circling around as they performed their rustic minuet, the music punctuated by high-pitched cries and the stamp of clogs. I dimly remembered a dance known as the funky chicken that came and went back in the sixties; this must be the original version, I thought.

'Ah, *there* you are,' I heard, and turned to see Régis propped up against the counter of a stall, glass in one hand and a slice of sausage in the other. 'I was getting worried about you. I thought you'd been dragged off by one of those turkeys. Big brutes, aren't they? Here, have a glass of wine to settle your nerves.' He put a hand on my arm. 'And for God's sake don't start looking at your watch. You're not in England now.'

I can't help it, even after all these years. It's the guilty English reflex, formed in the days of licensing laws when pubs had restricted opening hours and drinking was permitted only at the government's discretion. 'Maybe just the one,' I said. Régis shook his head as he slid a glass of Beaujolais along the

counter, and we drank in silence for a few moments, watching the crowd.

The clog dancers, rosy-faced from their exertions, had taken a break. On a platform set up in the middle of the hall, a panel of chicken-fanciers took turns at the microphone, discussing plumage and unctuous flesh and reminding us all that the winner of the *Grand Prix* would be receiving a vase of Sèvres porcelain, donated by the president of France. In return, the president would be sent a capon, which, according to Régis, would undoubtedly be awarded the Légion d'honneur. Posthumously, of course. 'And why not?' Régis added. 'They gave one to Jerry Lewis.'

I could see signs that Régis was ready to settle in for the rest of the morning, his elbow cocked comfortably on the bar, his hand moving hopefully in the direction of another glass of Beaujolais. It was now or never if we wanted to see the rest of the show. With a sigh of reluctance, he allowed himself to be led off to the hall of the dead.

It was a stunning sight. Row upon orderly row of immaculate corpses – something over a thousand, we were told – were lying in state on tables stretching from one end of the hall to the other. Members of the public filed past quietly, much in the style of mourners at a ceremonial funeral, their voices hushed and reverential as they commented on the extraordinary care and skill that had gone into the presentation.

Each chicken had its own shroud of what looked like fine white muslin, its feet folded beneath its stomach, the muslin sewn tight so that the body resembled a smooth oval cushion, but a cushion with a difference, having a neck and head protruding from one end. The neck feathers were left unplucked to form a handsome snowy ruff, and the resulting work of art – for that's how it looked – had been placed on its own white pad.

The birds had been decorated according to sex and racial status. Chickens wore slim ribbons of pale pink, tied with a bow around the breast, capons wore blue, turkeys sported a broader scarlet sash. All of them displayed the blue, white and red medals of Bresse. No mummy of ancient Egypt could have been more elegantly prepared for the hereafter than these birds, and I found it difficult to imagine eating them. They were more suitable for framing.

At a smaller table set apart from the others, a silver-haired lady with a dead chicken on her lap and astonishingly nimble fingers was demonstrating the finer points of making the ultimate outfit. She emphasized to us that the sewing she was doing so deftly was '*comme le lacement d'un corset*', or, for those of us unfamiliar with the lacing of corsets, cross-stitching. Once she was satisfied with her needlework, the chicken would be immersed in cold water. This, she told us, has the effect of shrinking the cotton to achieve an even snugger fit, at the same time squeezing the body within, which apparently does wonders for the texture of the skin by the time the bird reaches the dinner table. Not for the first time, I was amazed at Gallic attention to detail in service of the stomach.

That afternoon, as we were driving back from Bourg, Régis took what I thought was rather unnecessary pleasure in describing, with many chauvinistic asides, what we had just seen. Nowhere else in the world would one find such noble chickens, so nobly treated, he declared. Once again, French supremacy had been demonstrated. How fortunate I was, a mere foreigner, to be living in God's own country. And so on and on and on.

After half an hour of this relentless crowing, I'd had enough, and I thought it was time to remind Régis of a legend that, so far at least, the French have been unable to suppress.

The story goes that the bounties of France were deeply resented by her neighbours, the other Europeans. Eventually, jealous of such an overprivileged country, they got together in a rare moment of unity and decided to send their representatives to God in order to protest.

'You have given France the best of everything,' they said. 'The Mediterranean sea, the Atlantic ocean, mountains and fertile valleys, southern sunshine and romantic northern winters, a supremely graceful language, cooking rich with the finest butter and olive oil, the most varied and productive vineyards on earth, more cheeses than there are days in the year – everything, in fact, that man could desire, and all in one country. Is this fair? Is this Divine Justice?'

God listened to their complaints, considering them carefully. Thinking it over, He was obliged to admit that the protesters had a point. It was possible that He had been rather generous – perhaps overgenerous – to this blessed patch called France. And so, to make up for all those unfair advantages, God created the French. The other Europeans went home happy. Justice had been served.

Régis sniffed, one of those eloquent, disdainful French sniffs. 'Very droll,' he said. 'I suppose that would appeal to the English sense of humour.'

'Actually, it was a German friend who told me the story. He thought it was funny, too.'

Another sniff. 'What do you expect from someone who likes dumplings and sauerkraut?' He pushed back his seat and composed himself for sleep. Even his snores had a faintly supercilious sound about them. I don't know why I like him so much.

11

The guided stomach

Advice to the motorist in search of a room for the night:

Stop at the door of the hotel, and instruct the porter to leave your bags in the car. Make sure you discuss personally with the hotel proprietor the matter of his prices. If you judge them to be fair, but before committing yourself, demand to see the room he wants to give you. It is in his interest to fill his worst rooms first. If you are not convinced by the famous phrase 'We don't have anything else! We're completely full!' return to your car and make as if to go elsewhere. Nine times out of ten, at this precise moment, the hotel proprietor, smiting his forehead with his hand, will find quite by chance an excellent room that was vacated just an hour ago, and which he has completely overlooked . . .

A new century was dawning. Paris was preparing for the World's Fair, some cars had attained dizzying speeds well in excess of ten miles per hour, hotel owners were notorious for their dramatic habit of smiting their foreheads, and it was recommended that the comfort-conscious traveller check his room for fleas before settling down for the night. It was 1900, the year of the first Michelin guide to France, from which the extract above is taken.

It is a pocket-sized volume, this first edition, of just under four hundred tightly-set, busy-looking pages, and it was given away to owners of *voitures*, *voiturettes* and even *vélocipèdes* by the brothers Michelin. They had created the removable pneumatic tyre in 1891, and the guide was their way of encouraging motorists to wear out as much rubber as possible by extending their travels throughout France.

Car manufacturers, most of them long since gone, were permitted in those days to advertise in the pages of the guide, and we find the Rochet & Schneider two-seater – *robuste, simple, confortable, élégante, silencieux* – sharing space with the larger Schaudel, shown fully equipped with four men in peaked hats gazing out sternly over the facial topiary of their moustaches. One of the few advertisers whose name we would recognize today is Peugeot, although a hundred years ago, the Peugeot speciality was not the car but the folding bicycle, constructed in accordance with '*Le système du Capitaine Gerard*,' a pioneer in the field of bicycle-folding.

Nearly sixty of the opening pages in that first guide were devoted to explaining the marvels of the pneumatic tyre: its cushioned ride, its valves and grommets, its optimum levels of inflation, its care and repair. Other technical information took up more than a hundred pages at the back. In the middle was the filling in the sandwich, a listing of cities, towns and villages arranged in alphabetical order from Abbeville to Yvetot.

Beneath each listed place was its distance by road from the hub of the universe, Paris, or from the closest large town. The number of inhabitants was also recorded, although I've never worked out why that should be of any particular interest to motorists. And on every one of those cramped, old-fashioned pages can be seen early examples of a visual vocabulary that is now in its second century, Michelin sign language: a miniature chateau to indicate a hotel, a first aid cross for a resident doctor, a set of apothecary scales for a pharmacy, a tiny envelope for a post office, a steam engine for a station – even a black lozenge for hotels equipped with photographic darkrooms.

Darkrooms were rare, and so apparently were some other less artistic refinements. A note in the foreword tells the traveller that next year's guide would come to grips with the gurgling wonders of twentieth-century plumbing. Not only would hotels be credited for having bathrooms and showers, but also '*si les W.C. sont perfectionés avec un appareil de*

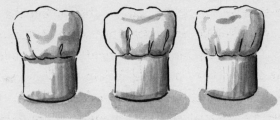

chasse' – if they have lavatories that flush – those, too, would be given the prominence they deserve.

Readers of that first guide were invited to write to Michelin with their comments, and they could hardly fail to have been impressed by the fund of technical and geographical information contained in the little book. But how many of them, I wonder, wrote in to ask that burning question so close and dear to any French heart at any time, but even more so after a hard day on the road. *What's for dinner?*

Because although hotels were listed, restaurants weren't. The guide was, after all, intended to be a survival manual for motorists driving primitive machinery that frequently broke down. A man whose valves and grommets were giving him trouble could hardly be expected to give much thought or attention to a menu. Heretical though it may sound, in those early years, mechanics were more important than chefs.

This changed by 1920. Cars had become more reliable and pneumatic tyres were no longer the novelty they had been twenty years before. Food, however, would never lose its charm, and perhaps it was this that prompted the Michelin brothers to make three fundamental – and, as it turned out, very astute – decisions about their guide that year: it should include restaurants; it should be sold in bookstores, rather than be given away; and it should no longer accept advertising.

It wasn't long before the restaurant listings, not surprisingly, began to overtake tips on tyre pressure as a reason for buying the guide. Every year, more restaurants were included, and naturally – like everything in France from suppositories to gravel – they had to be graded. More sign language was needed to identify the different levels of cooking skill – a short, simple way to let the wandering motorist know what he could expect to find on his plate. And not only *What's for dinner?* but also *How good will it be?* To answer these questions, the star system was born in 1926.

The Michelin stars, stylized rosettes that are called 'macaroons' by the pros of the industry, are the gold medals of kitchen Olympics. They are awarded, confirmed, or withdrawn every year. Winning a star can lift a young chef from obscurity overnight, giving him (or, less frequently, her) a reputation that extends to wherever the guide is sold and food is discussed. Losing a star is *catastrophique*, a professional disaster, a personal tragedy, a reason to smite the forehead, tear out the hair, and consider taking up a less demanding occupation.

What has always struck me about these annual dramas, which are widely reported in France, is that, in the most important sense, the decisions made by the guide are accepted. People may disagree – in fact, as it is France and as it concerns the stomach, they invariably *do* disagree – about a star being given or taken away. But I have never known anyone to accuse the guide of unfairness or bias. It is trusted.

I find this remarkable in a world where corruption is constantly being uncovered and is now more or less taken for granted in every activity from politics to bicycle racing.

One of the reasons the guide has managed to retain its virtue as well as its authority is the self-imposed ban on advertising that is now in its eighty-first year. Thanks to that ban, the guide contains none of the corporate graffiti that decorates almost everything we watch or read. I can think of hundreds of companies that would fall over themselves to advertise in the guide's closely studied pages: anyone selling food, drink, travel, kitchen equipment, cars, indigestion remedies, wonder diets – the list is long, and potentially very, very lucrative. The Michelin people could make a fortune. It does them credit that they prefer to maintain their independence and keep the guide commercial-free.

But the real strength of the guide is its system of restaurant evaluation, and the mysterious band of men and women who work within that system. These are the inspectors, *les incognitos*, whose names are never announced, whose photographs are never taken, and whose considerable talents are only recognized by a few souls of discretion in the Michelin head office.

The inspectors' method of working is a complete contradiction of the tactics normally practiced by food critics, who, with one or two exceptions, know more about self-promotion than cooking. Most food critics, I suspect, want to be known, to be recognized, to be stroked, to feel that their names send a *frisson* of apprehension up and down the chef's spine. A measure of celebrity, and the special attention it generates, is what they like when they eat. And restaurants should behave accordingly, if they know what's good for them. Waiters, many waiters, should flurry around. New off-menu dishes should be sent to the table for sampling. Chefs should drop by at the end of the meal to give away recipe secrets that will be published in the eventual review as the critic's own expert and perceptive discoveries. 'To my surprise, I detected a daring but successful touch of truffled apricots in the galantine of pork.' That sort of thing.

In contrast, the Michelin inspector's approach to a restaurant is the same as that of any normal customer. When he makes his reservation, his name doesn't ring any bells in the kitchen. (Even France's highly tuned network of gossip among chefs hasn't yet managed to identify inspectors, for reasons we shall come to later.) When the inspector arrives at the restaurant, he continues to make himself unknown. He doesn't ask for any particular table. He doesn't drop any hints to the headwaiter. He doesn't demand to meet the chef. He eats, he drinks, he pays his bill, and he leaves. And nobody in the restaurant, or the kitchen, is any the wiser.

There are people – my friend Régis, the glutton in chief, is one – who will tell you that eating for a living is as close as one can reasonably come to heaven on earth. He thinks he would love to be a Michelin inspector. And on the face of it, a career of being fed and watered by some of the world's best cooks does sound more attractive than chartered accountancy or commodities trading or, indeed, most other jobs. But is it? Does our inspector spring from his bed salivating every morning? Does he have a remedy for the gourmet's occupational ailment, the *crise de foie*? Where does he eat on his days off? Is he fat? I thought it would be fascinating to find out. And since I didn't know an inspector, or anybody who knew one, I decided that the only place to go for enlightenment was to taste bud headquarters, the Michelin office in Paris.

It is on the wide and leafy Avenue de Breteuil in the seventh *arrondissement*, a ten-minute stroll from my favourite food shop, the Bon Marché Grande Epicerie in the Rue du Bac. The Michelin building is set back from the street, functional and unremarkable, guarded by a sentry-box where visitors are required to state their business before being allowed in. My appointment was with Monsieur Arnaud, one of whose burdens in life it is to deal with nosy interlopers like myself.

He met me in the reception area, a dark-haired, distinguished man with a diplomatic air, and led me through a labyrinth of corridors to a small book-lined office. He gave me a shot of triple-strength coffee before asking how he could help.

'I'm fascinated by your team of inspectors,' I said.

He nodded amiably. I had the feeling this wasn't the first time he'd heard that.

'And what I'd really like is to have lunch with one of them.'

The Arnaud eyebrows went up. The Arnaud lips were pursed. 'That, I'm afraid, would be very difficult.'

'How about dinner?'

He smiled and shook his head. I didn't think it was worth suggesting breakfast.

'The problem is,' Arnaud said, 'that our inspectors must remain anonymous if they are to do their job properly.'

I told him I had no wish to blow an inspector's cover, but Arnaud remained adamant; polite, friendly, understanding, but adamant. It couldn't be done. And then he explained why.

Inspecting restaurants for Michelin is not an occasional diversion for people with an educated palate who like to eat, but a full-time, long-term, salaried career. Inspectors have usually had eight to ten years of experience working in the hotel or restaurant business – 'a basic education,' Arnaud called it – before joining Michelin. Then there is a training period of two years before they go out on the road to eat in earnest.

And when they do go out on the road, they're kept hard at it, weekends included: two meals a day, but never at the same type of restaurant, so that a two-star lunch may be followed by dinner in a bistro. During a typical week, inspectors will sample ten to fourteen kinds of cuisine. Two weeks of this, and then they will go back to Paris to write their reports. To make sure their faces don't become familiar in one particular area, they constantly switch regions, travelling about twenty thousand miles a year. Every starred restaurant will be visited and reviewed half a dozen times in the course of a year by different inspectors.

Reeling from this barrage of information, I asked what I thought was a harmless question. 'How many inspectors are there?'

Another enigmatic smile. I was trying to venture into forbidden territory.

'*Un certain nombre*,' said Arnaud. 'Enough to do the work.'

'And what do you look for in an inspector?'

'Discretion, both in manner and appearance. We don't want

anyone flamboyant, or too distinctive. We look for *Monsieur Tout le Monde*, Mr Everyman.'

That puts Régis out of the running, I thought. The last time I'd seen him, he'd been swirling through the village in a calf-length Tyrolean cloak, basketball boots, and a wide-brim Borsalino fedora, his cigar belching chimney-sized puffs of smoke. He is not the most unobtrusive of men.

Arnaud continued. 'Inspectors must, of course, be physically sound. They must have an exceptional sense of taste, and this must be educated enough to recognize if a chef has taken shortcuts. Or worse' – Arnaud's expression became grave – 'if he has been cheating.' He paused to let this horror sink in. 'Disguised dishes,' he said. 'Cod masquerading as another fish under the cover of a distracting sauce. Mutton dressed up as lamb. These things happen. Our man must be watchful. He must be able to see through the disguise without having to question the chef. One can never question the chef, because this is *un métier très discret*.'

Discretion was a recurring theme, and indeed Arnaud himself was proving to be as discreet as an oyster, although he did open up a little when we talked about female inspectors. They often notice details, he said, that men overlook. Only the other day he had been to lunch at a starred restaurant with a female inspector colleague, *Madame Tout le Monde*. He had found everything as it should be. Madame hadn't. She had noticed that one of the waiters had fingernails that were, shall we say, not quite *comme il faut*, not quite in the state of blanched and spotless, buffed perfection that they should be. Not the worst of crimes perhaps; not enough to strip away the stars. But a black mark nevertheless, and something that would be on the checklist for the next inspector.

There was no point, I knew, in asking what inspectors said about their work to their friends. Presumably they couldn't admit to the truth. Was there an approved Michelin cover story, backed up by a fake office and a secretary trained in the arts of espionage? Did the husbands and wives of inspectors know? What did they tell *their* friends? How did inspectors describe their occupation in the endless forms that one is required to fill out in France? The more I thought about it, the more it seemed like life in the witness protection pro-gramme, but with better food.

I left the Michelin building a wiser man, any illusions I might have had about the joys of eating for a living dispelled. An inspector's life was not for me. In fact, it sounded like a con-stant nightmare of self-restraint. There he is, our friend *Monsieur Tout le Monde*, cast adrift every lunchtime in a sea of temptation – exquisite food, fifty-page wine lists thick with cobwebbed treasures, deferential service, comfortable surroundings, no pressing appointments except dinner that evening – there he is, at the very pinnacle of civilized refreshment, and what does duty require him to do? Hold back. Concentrate. Take mental notes. Check the waiter's fingernails. Keep a sharp eye out for disguised dishes. *Work*.

Even when I was in the advertising business during those palmy days when the industry motto was 'Let's have lunch!' and the road to success was strewn with menus, I was never able to come to terms with the working lunch. For me, work and lunch are two activities that were never meant to co-exist and should never be forced to do so. Lunch is – or it should be – a pleasure. The wine and conversation should flow, the chef's efforts should be given the attention they deserve. Enjoyment should reign. How can this possibly happen if one is expected to discuss sales and distribution plans or the latest surgings and plummetings of the stock market, or even if, as with *Monsieur Tout le Monde*, lunch is something to be analyzed, dissected, judged, and pigeonholed? It flies in the face of nature. But although I could never do that, I am profoundly grateful to those who can, because they have laboured long and hard to produce the definitive bible of the belly.

There are, of course, many other food guides besides the Michelin. Some are good, some are cobbled together by enthusiastic amateurs, and some are not much more than vehicles for liquor advertising. None of them can match the Michelin recipe of impartiality, scope, professional attention to detail, and accuracy. (The town maps in the 1939 guide were so accurate they were used by the Allied forces in 1944 during the liberation of France.) And no other guide is as popular.

For once, this is not just my own highly subjective opinion. Statistics are on my side. *Le Guide Rouge 2000* had a first printing of 880,254 individually numbered copies, an enormous print run for a hard cover book. It was an immediate best-seller. As I write this, I have my copy (number 304,479) in front of me. It is a cheerfully coloured, reassuringly plump volume that makes its ancestor from 1900 look undernourished, even anorexic. This year, there are more than seventeen hundred pages listing more than five thousand hotels and more than four thousand restaurants. Adding to the volume's bulk is a Michelin novelty: for the first time in a hundred years, the sign language for each listing is amplified by descriptive text. A couple of sentences, no more. But we can imagine the months, perhaps years, of judicious pondering over at taste bud headquarters before the decision was taken to add words to pictograms, because one doesn't tamper lightly with an institution.

My only reservation about the guide is the effect it sometimes has on restaurants. I believe it tends to bring out the interior decorator that can occasionally be found lurking in the subconscious of some otherwise level-headed chefs. Let a star be awarded, and suddenly amid all the celebrations and cries of hail to the chef, through the joyous mist of champagne bubbles, the proprietor glances fondly around the restaurant and notices that there's . . . *something not quite right*. It is, he eventually realizes, the look of the place: the furniture, the accessories, the overall style of the room. They just won't do any more. They're too . . . well, too *ordinary* for an establishment that has now been elevated to the gastronomic heights. The restaurant has a macaroon, for heaven's sake! *Haute cuisine* deserves nothing less than *haut décor*. There's nothing for it but to call in the refurbisher.

And so those old, simple chairs are replaced by high-backed thrones covered in thick-cut, sumptuous bas-relief tapestry that costs more per square metre than foie gras. As for those serviceable plates and glasses, those unremarkable knives and forks, they must go, too. Bring on the Limoges and the Baccarat and the cutlery that looks as though it has come straight out of the presidential dining room in the Élysée Palace. Soon there is fine linen for the tables, silver-topped crystal decanters for the wine, great shiny domes to protect the food during its brief journey from kitchen to customer. And finally, let's smarten up the staff by putting them in new outfits – something sleek and chic and, more often than not, black.

This is all well and good if it stops there; a facelift, nothing more. Alas, there are times when it changes not just the appearance of the restaurant but its personality as well. Eminence breeds reverence, and what was once a comfortable, easy-going place becomes, in that ominous and overused phrase, a temple of gastronomy. A shrine. Not only that; the investment required for thrones and domes and decanters and designer plates is colossal, which puts a severe additional pressure on the poor man in the kitchen whose cooking has to pay for it all.

I've wondered many times over the years why an accolade for excellent cooking should lead to a frenzy of redecoration, and not long ago I had the chance to ask a local chef about it. He has recently been attracting a lot of well-deserved attention; his food is terrific, and his restaurant is delightful. It won't be long before he gets his first star. I think he sees it as a mixed blessing.

Of course, he would be thrilled. For a chef, Michelin stars are the stuff of dreams. But certain improvements would have to be made, he said, as we looked around the room where I have spent many happy and well-fed hours; a friendly room, where you feel at home as soon as you sit down.

'Why change anything?' I said.

He shrugged. 'Customers expect it. What can I do?'

Then I understood. It wasn't an edict handed down by Michelin. It wasn't the chef's desire to improve his working scenery. This whole thing – the summoning of the refurbisher, the Élysée Palace cutlery, the new ensembles for the staff – is all done to satisfy a deeply felt need in the French psyche that I've noticed before: the passion for trappings, the love of *luxe*. Who knows how it began? It might well have been started by the courtiers at Versailles, who were always trying to keep up with each other in the matter of velveteen breeches, scented gloves, hand-knitted wigs, and other items of conspicuous consumption. In any case, it was subsequently adopted with tremendous gusto by the prosperous members of the *bourgeoisie* – the kind of people who today buy La Cornue stoves and Hermes picnic baskets; the kind of people who have the money and the inclination to eat out frequently; the kind of people, in other words, who make restaurants successful and profitable.

They insist on their comforts, according to my friend the chef, and you will never hear them complain about a surfeit of upholstery, an excess of crystal, or too many waiters. In fact, as he said, that is what they expect from a restaurant when it has reached a certain level. A little pomp is necessary. The food is crucial, certainly, but so are the surroundings. Success in the kitchen must be reflected by the trappings of success in the dining room. Otherwise, apparently, customers will feel let down. Or even worse, some of the more sensitive among them might have the terrible suspicion that they're paying one-star prices to eat in a homely old bistro.

It's a difficult, demanding business running a top restaurant, and one that requires a particular mixture of talents. Part artist, part sergeant-major, part diplomat; the great chefs have to be all of these, and they can't afford to have off days, because someone – possibly *Monsieur Tout le Monde* himself – will be watching. France's longest-serving three-star chef, Paul Bocuse, received his stars back in 1965, and he still has them today. Thirty-five years without putting a foot wrong in the kitchen. The man deserves a medal for stamina.

And so do some of the other veterans. Looking through the pages of the 2000 edition, you will find 116 establishments, identified by a laurel wreath surrounding the magic number 100, that were recommended in the original guide a century ago. One of these monuments happens to be the Hôtel d'Europe in Avignon, not far from us, and we thought it would be interesting to see how it was holding up under the weight of all those years.

In fact, the hotel was doing brisk business long before the Michelin brothers discovered it. Built in the sixteenth century, it was acquired by a widow, Madame Pierron, who opened her doors to travellers in 1799. Bigwigs of every description came to stay: cardinals and archbishops, princes and statesmen, even Napoleon Bonaparte. History doesn't relate whether Joséphine came too, but it seems he had fond memories of the place. When he was fighting in Russia, surrounded by officers complaining about the discomforts of war, he showed little sympathy. '*Sacré bleu!*' he is reported to have said, 'we're not at Madame Pierron's hotel.'

He would have no difficulty recognizing it today. It's on one of the prettiest squares in Avignon, the Place Crillon, just inside the ramparts that have protected the centre of town for six hundred years. The classical architecture of the *place* has survived without too much interference from town planners, the street is still cobbled, and the hotel's handsome façade remains simple, without any of the neon trimmings that disfigure so many old buildings.

After passing through an entrance wide and high enough for a coach and horses, we found ourselves in a huge paved courtyard. There were trees, flowers, a fountain, and a smiling manager at the door. Already, I could see why Napoleon liked staying here. He would have liked our room, too, with its view across tiled rooftops towards the floodlit Palais des Papes. And he would undoubtedly have liked the cooking.

We sat over a long dinner, made longer by the generosity of the chef. He has one Michelin star, and he is pursuing a second with an enthusiasm that spilled over on to our plates. We ordered three courses and ended up tasting six – only tasting, because the three extra surprises were no more than a couple of perfectly presented mouthfuls; just enough to keep the palate sharp without blunting the appetite. It was the next best thing to being invited into the kitchen.

The hours went by, leaving the restaurant almost empty except for our invisible companions, the ghosts of those who had eaten there over the past two centuries: Grand Duke Vladimir of Russia, Charles Dickens, John Stuart Mill, Robert

Browning and Elizabeth Barrett during their elopement, Chateaubriand, the future king Edward VII – and, blending into the background as they kept a careful eye on everything from the waiter's fingernails to the chef's sauces, several generations of Michelin inspectors.

It had been a lovely evening, and it marked the end of a certain stage in the preparation of this book – the end of that leisurely, enjoyable and often well-fed process that I like to call research. A toast seemed appropriate.

We drank to chefs, particularly French chefs. And then we raised our glasses again to that unsung hero of the table, custodian of the nation's stomach and seeker after gastronomic immortality, wherever he can find it: *Monsieur Tout le Monde*. Let's hope he's with us for another hundred years.

12

A civilized purge

IT IS ASTONISHING how many experts there seem to be nowa-days whose mission in life is to lecture us about the perils of pleasure. Scarcely a week goes by without some ominous pronouncement about the price we must pay for our brief moments of indulgence. Even moderation, which used to be an acceptable excuse for the beef on your plate or the wine in your glass, is no longer good enough. If we are to believe some of the more extreme disciples of clean living, the only sure salvation for the human body is almost complete denial; no red meat, no butter, no cheese, no fat of any kind, no alcohol, no sugar, no tobacco, no direct sunlight.

I'm a sitting target for the health vigilantes, since three of my favourite sins are wine, a certain amount of fat in the diet, and lying in the sun. These are the habits of a man whose days are numbered. I have this on the authority of our friend Odile, the harbinger of gloom. Strangely enough, I like Odile. She is a good-looking, charming woman, splendid in every respect, except for her well-meaning but infuriating attempts to save me from my wicked ways. She appointed herself some years ago as my gastronomic conscience, and there was even a time when she urged me to follow her example. Here, I have to say, she practises what she preaches. She leads a life of shining intestinal virtue: water by the bucketful, herbal infusions, biologically active yoghurt, brown rice, soy milk, shoots and sprouts, one naughty glass of red wine a week, frequent days of fasting. It is a regime that suits her. For some extraordinary reason, she thinks it would suit me as well, if only I would give it a try.

When I started to work on this book, her murmurs of concern about my dreadful habits turned into cries of alarm. To go around France eating and drinking and, no doubt, carousing? Madness! Suicide by knife and fork! I tried to explain to Odile that it was research, no more than a professional necessity, but she wasn't fooled. She preferred to see it as an invitation to wretched excess: a surfeit of food, a torrent of alcohol, a death knell for the liver. There was only one hope for me, she said, and that was to end my research – if indeed I survived – with a period of exile in a spa, where a thorough cleansing of my internal workings could be carried out under professional, medically approved conditions. I would eat sparingly. I would turn my back on the grape. I would flush my toxins out with water. With luck, I would be saved.

The idea wasn't appealing. I had never been to a spa before, but in my ignorance I was sure I knew what to expect: expensive suffering. I anticipated a diet of roots and berries and bean curd, strange leafy drinks, high colonics, savage bouts of exercise under the supervision of perfectly formed, tireless human robots – in other words, the boot camp system, based on the premise that the treatment can't be doing you any good unless it is humiliating, foul-tasting, and painful. I foresaw starvation, sweat, guilt, and discomfort in equal doses, and at the end of it all a bill to curdle your newly purified blood. A truly hellish prospect, and I was determined to have nothing to do with it.

But I had reckoned without my wife. She has an admirably open mind about health and nutrition, and she is quite happy to experiment with anything from ginseng root to royal jelly and tofu tips. She liked the idea of a few days in a spa. She thought it would certainly be good for us and might even be enjoyable. 'Don't forget,' she said, 'it would be a French spa. And you know what the French are like.'

Yes indeed; a people not noted for holding back when it comes to food and drink, or famous for their love of exercise. On the other hand, they have a deep fondness for *luxe et volupté*, for coddling themselves inside and out. The Anglo-Saxon idea of the boot camp route to health is alien to them, and it would send them rushing in the opposite direction, probably to dive into a five-course meal. For a spa to succeed in France, it would have to cater to French tastes and appetites, and therefore even I would find it quite acceptable. So ran the argument. Eventually, I was convinced. Now all we had to do was find the spa with the best chef.

I have no doubt there are good chefs working in spas throughout France, but the godfather of them all is Michel Guérard, one of the first modern celebrity cooks. He became a household name in France more than twenty years ago when he invented *Cuisine Minceur*. This was based on the thought – revolutionary in those days, and not all that common even now – that a regime could actually be pleasant. You should be able to eat real food, drink a little wine, refresh your system, and take some pleasure from the normally dreary process of inner cleansing and weight loss.

The test of Guérard's delightful theory, obviously, was how this magical diet tasted. Was *Cuisine Minceur* really delicious? And was there enough of it, or did you leave the table sucking your napkin, with your stomach growling for *steak frites*? The answers to these questions have clearly been favourable, because Guérard and his cuisine have prospered enormously over the years. His establishment at Eugénie les Bains, about a two-hour drive south of Bordeaux, is one of the best-known spas in Europe, and the restaurant is one of only twenty-two in France to have been awarded three Michelin stars.

I kept that thought in mind as we were driving through the pine forests towards Eugénie, ready to be cosseted and restored to perfect health. I had spent a gruelling year with knife, fork, and corkscrew, and to be put on a diet by a three-star chef would be a fitting end to my research. The sun was shining, anticipation was doing wonders for my appetite, and the only small cloud on the horizon was the realization that we were going to be late for lunch. So late, in fact, that lunch was probably out of the question.

And so it would have been, I believe, in most hotels or restaurants (even in France, where there is an instinctive sympathy for the empty belly). But within minutes of checking in, well past lunchtime, we were sitting on the terrace outside our room, where a table had been smothered in white linen, decorated with fresh flowers, and equipped with all the essentials for a comfortable afternoon: an ice bucket with a bottle of chilled white Bordeaux, generous servings of foie gras, a plate of local cheeses, salad, and a large bowl of raspberries on a bed of chopped strawberries. At a stroke, I felt my misgivings about spas begin to melt away. Perhaps I'd been a little hasty in my rush to judgement. This was certainly no hardship.

Our programme of treatments – *la cure* – didn't begin until the following morning, and so, once the foie gras had settled we had a chance to inspect our surroundings. We were staying in a building tucked away in the hotel grounds, a restored eighteenth-century convent, built in the shape of an E around a charming garden and a tiny fountain. In our room, there were exposed beams, polished flagstones, oriental rugs, a large canopied bed and – most unusual in France – a vast bathroom with a powerful shower and a tub easily big enough for two. There were tulips and roses. There were linen sheets as crisp and smooth as new five-hundred-franc notes. There

was, just a short stroll away, the kitchen of one of the most
eminent cooks in the world. The whole place oozed with *luxe
et volupté*, and I had some difficulty persuading my wife to
venture outdoors so that we could take a look at the rest of
the spa.

The main building is a sweeping, elegant affair, and contains other guest apartments, the kitchens and the restaurant.
There are none of the obvious signs or smells of a health
resort – no insufferably perky instructors with clipboards and
stopwatches and paramedical uniforms, no panting guests in
workout clothes, none of the antiseptic, self-righteous whiff I
had always associated with premises dedicated to physical
improvement.

It wasn't until we walked across the gardens to *La Ferme
Thermale* that there was any intimation of spa life, and even
this was presented with considerable restraint and style.
Outside, the building looked like a classic eighteenth-century
wood-framed farmhouse; inside, beams and plaster gave way
to marble and tiles and more than three thousand square feet
of assorted aids to feeling immortal – or at least feeling a little
thinner, cleaner and more relaxed.

Young ladies in white were gliding in and out of various
treatment rooms with their clients, some of whom looked
rather apprehensive in their linen robes, as though they feared
that public nudity was just around the corner. Other clients
were fortifying themselves between treatments with aromatic
teas in front of a huge fireplace in the main salon. Logs crack-
led discreetly in the hearth. Otherwise, the atmosphere was
serene, with not even the muted rumble of a *minceur* stomach

to disturb the calm. The next day, it would be our turn to plunge into the herbal jacuzzi, the hammam room, the mud bath, and the needle water-massage. Meanwhile, we had what remained of the afternoon to explore the village.

At last count, there were 507 inhabitants of Eugénie les Bains, and I suspect that a high proportion of them work in one way or another to attend to the well-being of visitors in search of internal improvement. This has officially been a healthy spot since 1843, when a licence was granted to exploit the waters. And there the village might have remained, little known and hidden away, except for two events that made it famous.

The first was in 1861, when the senior members of the commune decided that a little royal assistance would do wonders for the reputation of the local liquids. History doesn't relate exactly how the mayor pulled it off, but he managed to persuade the Empress Eugénie, wife of Napoleon III, to give not only her patronage but her name to the village. Overnight, the water was promoted from an everyday tipple to a noble elixir, suitable for the most aristocratic digestive systems.

And then, in 1975, Michel Guérard arrived. He had married a local girl, Christine Barthelemy, whose father owned the *Etablissement Thermal*. There was plenty of room for a kitchen. There was also an opportunity to provide food that complemented the water cure – something light, something healthy – something, in other words, like *Cuisine Minceur*.

Today, Eugénie calls itself France's premier *minceur* village. It has also been called 'Guérardville', because the maestro's influence is everywhere. There is the main hotel, the annex where we were staying, the thermal farm, a second, smaller hotel, another restaurant, a local vineyard. It is a small industry built on a paradox: eat, drink, and lose weight.

The light was fading as we sat outside the café on Eugénie's main street. A small and friendly place, it acts as an occasional refuge for those in need of a brief escape from the cure. Three people whom we had seen in the thermal spa had come into the café from the direction of the *boulangerie* a hundred yards away. They were nursing small paper bags. They looked around with furtive, sideways glances – the very essence of guilt – before ordering large cups of hot chocolate. With a final check to make sure there were no *minceur* officials watching, they unwrapped their tarts and almond biscuits and slices of cream cake, took that first rich, melting mouthful, raised their eyes in ecstasy, and sighed. Anyone would think they'd had nothing but nut cutlets for weeks. Would this be us in the days to come?

Suddenly hungry, we looked at each other and reviewed our options for dinner. In the hotel dining room, there was a choice between *Cuisine Minceur* (for the serious seekers after weight loss) or the longer and more robust *Menu Gourmand* (for writers doing research). Or there was Guérard's country restaurant, *La Ferme aux Grives*, a two-minute stroll from the hotel. We had already looked at the menu posted outside. It listed delights that we were sure would be frowned upon the next day. And then, we easily persuaded ourselves, was soon enough to start on the road to restraint.

The restaurant, in what was once a farmhouse, had the

feeling of an enormous kitchen. At one end of the room, a long butcher's table was piled with a landscape of fresh vegetables – peppers, leeks, tomatoes, white aubergines and crinkly, deep-green cabbages. Behind the vegetable panorama was a ten-foot-wide fireplace, where legs of lamb twisted slowly on a spit, their juices hissing as the drops fell on the fire, giving off the nostalgic scent of wood-roasted meat. We could hear above the ebb and flow of conversation the gentle creak and muffled pop of corks being eased out of bottles.

It was an ideal setting for our last supper, and the food lived up to the surroundings. We ate grilled leeks wrapped in a tissue of pink Bayonne ham, a perfectly grilled chicken with a crisp skin the colour of old gold, and – a final treat before the thin days to come – the pick of the cheese board. Let the following day bring what it may. At least we would meet it with contented stomachs.

Before going to the thermal farm the next morning I read through a different kind of menu, one that listed all the treatments from rejuvenating baths to a variety of massages tailored to different body parts. For the most beneficial results, according to the instructions, it was recommended that these activities should be performed *entièrement nu*, or naked as nature intended. I thought nothing of it at the time, but it came back to me a little later when we had changed into our linen robes and were waiting in the reception area for battle to commence. Looking around, I noticed a distinct imbalance in the sexes. There was not a single man on the spa staff. They were all young ladies; attractive, slim and amiable young ladies, and I was to deliver my body into their hands. I instinctively stood up straight and inhaled, hoping to disguise the effects of dinner the night before.

But there was nothing else to be done except lie back and enjoy whatever the young ladies had in mind, and as it happened, the first two or three treatments were carried out with a regard for modesty that would have made Queen Victoria nod with approval. I was taken to the doors of various rooms, told what to do and what to expect, and left alone with my nudity. The programme was so well organized and discreet, so private, that I might have been the only client in the spa.

I sweated in solitude, enveloped in the steam clouds of the hammam. I lay on a slab of heated marble for an overall herbal rinse – excellent for cellulite, so I was told – before moving on to a miniature swimming pool, where I was pummeled from neck to ankle by jets of thermal water. My cricks disappeared, my joints were eased, and my muscles became elastic. By the time I met my wife in the main salon, halfway through the morning, I was so relaxed I was having difficulty keeping my eyes open, and I nearly dropped off in the armchair while drinking a warm herbal *tisane*.

This mixture, tasting pleasantly of lemons and seemingly quite innocuous, is part of the inner purging process. '*Buvez et éliminez*' is the spa's motto, and they're not joking. In my case, the liquid had an almost instant eliminating effect on the bladder. It was a reaction that I learned to anticipate over the next few days, making sure I never drank any of these *tisanes* unless there was a bathroom within fifty yards. I even caught myself keeping an eye open on the way to and from our room for convenient clumps of shrubbery in case the great eliminator struck again.

After our first dose of this rather dramatic pick-me-up, it was time for my wife and me to share the next treatment. We were taken to a room with a sunken bath, big enough for half a dozen people, which was filled with a thick, opaque liquid. It was mud, but thermal mud, mud of great refinement, mud *de luxe*, somewhere in colour between off-white and the palest green. I had always thought of mud baths as barely one step up from the swamp – lumpy, gaseous, and noisome, bubbling with smells of rot. But this was as smooth as oil, inoffensive to the nose, and astonishingly buoyant.

We found that after a few minutes of experimental wallowing, we could float in a sitting position, knees drawn up, arms spread out for balance, while the mud went to work. And what therapeutic mud it was, according to the young lady in charge: wonderful for rheumatism, excellent for stress, and a godsend for anyone suffering from that popular malady the French describe so delicately as '*les problèmes de transit intestinal*'. On top of all that, it was an extraordinarily pleasant sensation, as though we had immersed ourselves in warm cream. We could happily have spent the rest of the morning bobbing around in it, half-standing, half-floating, slippery and weightless, giving not a thought to problems of *transit intestinal*.

After a shower, we went our separate ways: my wife to the heated marble slab, while I was led off by one of the young ladies in white to a large glass box. And there I stood, *entièrement nu* as she had instructed, spreadeagled against the glass wall, with my back to her. I looked over my shoulder with what I hoped was a nonchalant expression and asked the young lady, who was standing outside the box, what was going on. She smiled sweetly and adjusted the nozzle of a hose before aiming it at me through a hole in the glass.

'This is very good for toning the body and for *drainage*,' she said. 'First, I do your back part. When I tap on the wall, you turn sideways so that I can do your side part.'

I was still wondering whether my *drainage* was that obvious a problem when she let rip. For those of you who have never had a concentrated high-pressure massage, I can tell you that it is just this side of pain, a million liquid needles going up and down your body, from the calves to the base of the skull. In fact, it felt terrific, but I was glad I wasn't facing the other way.

After a few bracing minutes, there was a tap on the glass wall. I turned sideways. One hip, half a set of ribs, and a shoulder were made to tingle. Then another tap, so that the other side could be dealt with. I felt as rosy as a freshly cooked ham.

The jet stopped. I was just about to thank the young lady for a uniquely stimulating experience, when she tapped again. 'Now I do your front part,' she said.

The full monty.

It is a most curious feeling to stand naked, poised to flinch, facing a young woman you have only just met while she directs lethally powerful jets of water up and down your body. Not unpleasant by any means, but curious, and it poses one or two social questions. Should you attempt to make polite conversation, or would that distract her and put her off her aim, possibly with excruciating results? And what should you do with your hands? Should one assume the at-ease position, with hands clasped behind the back? The casual, full-disclosure pose, with hands on hips? Total surrender, with hands on the head? Or should the hands be on guard duty farther down? It was one of those moments that defies any attempt at sophisticated deportment. I wondered what Cary Grant, the king of savoir faire, would have done in similar circumstances.

I also wondered how the young lady would reply if she was at a party and someone asked her about her work.

'Tell me, what do you do for a living?'

'Oh, I put naked men and women up against a wall and give them hell with a high-pressure hose.'

By now, I had a full-body blush. Lingering traces of *drainage*, I was sure, would have been washed away, together with cellulite and any body hair and layers of epidermis that weren't securely anchored. But the sense of well-being was marvellous. My skin felt as though it had been sluiced down with champagne.

So ended the first morning, and it was remarkable how two and a half hours of treatments – a period during which I had done nothing more physically demanding than take off my clothes – could provoke such a ferocious appetite. As we were walking over to the hotel restaurant, fond memories of the previous night's dinner returned, only to be suppressed. Now we were in the grip of the cure. Now we were to experience our first encounter with *minceur* food, described in lyrical style by Guérard as *'une cuisine gaie, harmonieuse et savoureuse.'*

Before we had even reached our table, I was struck by one of the great joys of staying in a top-class hotel: life has no rough edges. You are surrounded by people who have been trained to please and, God bless them, they seem to enjoy doing it. As we were escorted through the lobby, we were greeted by smiles, inquiries after our health and a salvo of *bons appétits.* We felt welcome. We felt loved. Above all, we felt hungry.

The fact that we kept to our original high-minded intentions and chose the *minceur* menu instead of the gourmet's special is a tribute to my wife's willpower rather than mine. I have a tendency to waver at the prospect of lobster and truffled titbits. She is made of stronger stuff. Also, as an accomplished cook herself, she was fascinated to see what Guérard could do with fewer calories than a cheeseburger and french fries.

Minceur cooking, if you should want to try it yourself, is based on a few simple principles: use plenty of fruit and vegetables; replace butter and cream with olive and colza oils; replace synthetic sugar with natural fructose; prepare a lighter meal – usually fish – in the evening, for a thinner dinner; and drink wine every day. So much for the rules. Stick to those, and produce meals that look and taste like the very best three-star food. Nothing to it, really. All it takes is a prodigious amount of time and talent.

Ignoring the example of the couple at the next table, who had ordered two different types of mineral water, I asked for the permitted glass of red wine, and we set to. There were three courses in that first lunch, and they bear describing in some detail.

First was a broth made with mussels, carrots, garlic, mushrooms, olive oil and white wine. The flavour was intense and rich, and I felt sure that someone must have slipped a dollop of cream into the recipe while the chef wasn't looking. But no; the calorie count was 165, about the same as a small pot of low-fat yoghurt. The broth was followed by a vegetable risotto – rice from the Camargue cooked in chicken stock with peas, shallots, baby onions, and white and green beans – a moist and glorious mixture served with a dusting of fresh Parmesan. Calories: 240, slightly fewer than a bar of chocolate. Finally, the most delicate combination of tastes: raspberries, strawberries and blackcurrants bathed in a light fructose syrup and topped with ice cream made from yoghurt and *fromage blanc*. Calories: 95.

Including the glass of red wine, the entire lunch added up to fewer than six hundred calories. It had been beautifully presented and served, and it was delicious. But what impressed us as much as anything else was the feeling that we had eaten a satisfying meal. We had no pangs of deprivation, and it was hard to believe that food of this astonishingly high

standard was part of a health cure. Here was a diet, my wife told me, that she would be happy to live with for a long time.

We sat over coffee and looked around at our fellow dieters. They were mostly French, with a sprinkling of Americans, and you could tell where they came from without hearing them speak. The Americans were consulting maps and guide-books and making notes. The French were studying the menus for dinner (480 calories for the *minceur* meal of soup, fish and sorbet, and a tactfully unspecified amount for the five-course gourmet's delight).

Over the next three days – which consisted of treatments and consistently superb food and an increasing sense of having left real life somewhere else – I was conscious of a change in my disposition. As a rule, I am terrible at vacations. I run out of books and boredom sets in, and then some faint, nagging echo of my Anglo-Saxon conscience tells me that I should be doing something useful, or at least active. But here, my daily responsibilities were limited to turning up on time at the thermal farm and raising an eager knife and fork twice a day in the restaurant. I was doing absolutely nothing and enjoying it, something that had never happened to me before. Perhaps it was the mud baths and the attentions of all those young ladies in white. Or maybe it was the total absence of any pressure to take part in conventional exertions. Tennis, swimming, cycling, hiking – these were all available, but we happily ignored them, quite content to be idle. And that, I suppose, is the great benefit of a civilized spa.

As if the rigours of everyday life at Eugénie were too much to bear without a period of recovery, the Guérards decided not long ago to open a rest camp by the sea. Their new outpost, the Domaine de Huchet, is on the Atlantic coast, about an hour and a half from the spa. It overlooks the longest beach in Europe – a wide, unbroken ribbon of smooth, clean sand that extends all the way from Arcachon in the north down to Biarritz. And there at Huchet we were promised three days of sea air and *farniente*, or lazing around, after our exhausting time dashing in and out of mud baths and needle showers.

Despite the map and the detailed instructions we'd been given, we were convinced we were lost as we turned off a road and on to a rutted earth track that disappeared into a dense pine forest. The ruts became deeper, the tunnel of trees closed in, and if the track had been wide enough we would have turned the car around. We must have made a mistake, we thought. This wasn't the middle of nowhere; it was the end of nowhere. But we pressed on, and after a mile or so, the trees thinned out and the sky reappeared. And there, perched on a dune, we could see a vast wooden house, immaculately painted in shades of sand and deep, faded red, a model of colonial architecture – low and square, with long verandas on two sides. In the area of flat land in front of the house were two other low buildings the colour of driftwood, each with a tiny fenced garden. A pathway made from slatted wood led through the dunes to the ocean, and we could hear the thump of surf as we got out of the car.

There was a welcoming committee of two. Martine and Max, the young couple in charge of Huchet, showed us around while explaining how we were going to keep body and soul together over the next three days. Every morning, *un brunch copieux* would be served in the dining room up until 11 a.m. Martine assured us that it would be more than enough to keep us going until 5.00 p.m., when there would be tea. Dinner at 7.30, courtesy of Max. 'It's not *minceur*,' he said, 'but it's healthy. I do a lot of grilling.' He pointed to his barbecue outside the kitchen door, an iron contraption that looked like the wheelbarrows used in the vineyards of Provence for burning clippings. That night's choice was either sea bass or breast of duck, with cream of potato and leek soup or foie gras to start and two desserts to finish. We thought we could forgive Max for not being a *minceur* cook.

We spent the afternoon exploring. The main house, which had been built in 1859 by a Bordelais baron as a hunting box, looked as though it had just been prepared for a photographer from *Interiors* or *Côté Sud* – an elegant series of rooms with four-poster beds, unfussy antique furniture, wood-burning fireplaces and stoves, and wide-plank floors of honey-coloured wood. It looked beautiful without being precious, and it gave you the feeling that you could actually live in it, which is not always the case with photogenic houses.

Outside, we followed the wooden pathway down to the Atlantic. We shared the beach with a solitary fisherman, thigh-deep in the foam, casting for bass. Otherwise, we had no company apart from seagulls. We could have walked a hundred kilometres in either direction and still been walking on sand. We could have swam westward towards America. Or, after a brisk half hour, we could have gone back to sit on the veranda, had tea, and watched the sun slide slowly down before dipping into the horizon. Not a difficult decision.

We had seen no other guests so far. Huchet can only take about half a dozen, and it wasn't until we went into the dining room for dinner that we met the only other couple staying there. We congratulated one another on our good luck at finding what they called '*paradis-sur-mer*', then sat down with a drink at our table in front of the fire. Like the rest of the house, the dining room was a study in comfortable good taste: a floor of putty-coloured flagstones, a ceiling with white-washed beams, the glow of candlelight on crystal glasses, linen tablecloth and napkins, bone china. The attention to detail was an example to any restaurant, let alone a tiny dining room hidden away behind God's back.

Looking through the glass door that opened on to a terrace, we could see Max hovering over his wheelbarrow barbecue with two long-handled forks, looking like a xylophone player in a chef's hat. Martine put another log on the fire, refilled our glasses, and opened the bottle of wine we were having with dinner. All was well with the world.

Max showed himself to be worthy of his hat, and a virtuoso on the barbecue. The breast of duck, a fan of pink slices on the plate, tasted of the outdoors: gamy, juicy, tender –

everything my efforts on the barbecue aspire to but never achieve. Maybe I should use aged wood and pine needles instead of charcoal. Maybe I should invest in a tall white hat. Or maybe I should spend years in Guérard's kitchens trying to learn what Max learned. He cooks all you eat at Huchet, from soups and flans to desserts and the pound cake served with afternoon tea. My wife wanted to take him home with us.

Dinner ended with cheese from the Pyrenees, followed by coffee and the favourite local sedative, a generous shot of Armagnac. This has been accurately described as brandy with a rustic character. It has a taste of caramel and a kick like a mule with a velvet hoof, and its immediate effect is eight hours of innocent slumber.

I was woken up by two seagulls having an argument outside the window, and I remembered that today we were planning to walk at least part of the way to Biarritz before attempting *le brunch*. The dunes were coated in the cotton-wool of an early morning sea-mist as we went down the path, a mist that muffled the surf the way a snowfall deadens the sounds of the countryside. A fisherman – perhaps the same optimist we had seen the day before – stood with his hands on his hips and the butt of his rod stuck in the sand, gazing intently at the waves, as though sea bass could be enticed out of the water by hypnosis.

We left the beach to follow a track through the tufts of sea-grass and into the dunes, carpeted as far as the eye could see with low-lying green scrub. There were no buildings, no telephone poles, no jarring signs of human interference, and we were reminded how easy it is in France (which has the same population as Britain, and three times the land-mass) to find great tracts of land where there is nothing but nature.

An hour's march later, the view was still the same green carpet, rolling down towards the Pyrenees. The sun had burned through the mist, and our calf muscles were beginning to ache from trudging through loose sand. We decided that Biarritz could wait. We had earned our breakfast.

Unlike the British and the Americans, who traditionally see their first meal of the day as a chance to top up their cholesterol levels, the French habitually do little more than nibble. Instead of eggs, bacon, sausage, beans, waffles and buttered toast, the Frenchman tends to confine himself to the three C's – coffee, croissants and cigarettes – conscious of the fact that he needs to be on form for lunch. (There is a theory that this is a poor start to the day, and that insufficient nutrition makes him bad-tempered until noon, but in my experience this applies only to café waiters and cab drivers.)

Breakfast at Huchet was, as Martine had promised, *copieux*: baked apples and yoghurt, eggs however we wanted them, plates of Bayonne ham and cheese, thick slices of grilled country bread, homemade jams from the kitchens at Eugénie, and two warm silver-wrapped packages the size of small loaves, the mother and father of all croissants, a good eight inches from nose to tail, plump, light, and buttery. No chewing required. They melted.

We rose to the challenge, then walked it off during the afternoon. And that was the pattern of our days at Huchet: sea air, glorious food, *farniente*. It had been a memorably pampered, well-fed week.

The morning after we got home, Odile called, curious to know if I had now been converted to the low-fat life.

'*Alors?* How was it? How do you feel?'

'Never felt better, Odile. Like a young sprig of eighteen. It was marvellous.'

'Did you lose weight?'

'I never weighed myself. But I'm relaxed, clear-eyed, bursting with health, ready for anything. And we never really felt hungry.'

'Ah, you see? It is just as I keep telling you. You have more sensible food, you cut out the wine, and *voilà*, you are a new man. Tell me, what did you eat?'

'Duck, lamb, guinea fowl, pâté, cheese, butter, eggs, a little foie gras, potato soup, *huge* croissants for breakfast . . .'

Silence on the other end of the line.

'. . . and there were some very nice little wines, too. And Armagnac. You should try it sometime. Do you the world of good.'

Odile laughed. '*Toujours l'humour anglais*. But seriously . . .'

Ah well. Sometimes, there's nothing as hard to swallow as the truth.

Last course

THERE IS ONLY so far descriptions on a page can go; nothing is quite like being there. And so, for those of you who would like to see for yourselves some of the restaurants, places and events that I've written about, here are a few details. I can't, unfortunately, give precise dates of the fairs and festivals, as these will change by a day or two each year, but I've included contact addresses where appropriate. Get in touch by phone or fax (much of rural France may not yet be plugged in to e-mail), and all will be revealed. The organizers of these events welcome a big turnout, and I've found that inquiries usually receive prompt and helpful replies. Good luck! I hope you have as much fun as I did.

The inner Frenchman

Marius et Janette, 4 Avenue Georges Cinq, Paris. Phone: 01.42.23.41.88. Fax: 01.47.23.07.19. One Michelin star. Specialities: Grilled sea bass, turbot *aioli* (garlic mayonnaise). L'Isle Sonnante, 7 Rue Racine, 8400 Avignon. Phone: 04.90.82.56.01. One Michelin star. Specialities: Filet of rabbit stuffed with olive purée, game and wild mushrooms in season. Restaurant La Fontaine, Place de La Fontaine, 84760 Saint Martin de La Brasque. Phone: 04.90.07.72.16.

For what we are about to receive

La messe des Truffes takes place on a Sunday during the second half of January. Contact: La Mairie, 84600 Richerenches. (The nearest big town is Orange.)

The thigh-tasters of Vittel

La Foire aux Grenouilles takes place towards the end of April. Contact: La Maison de Tourisme, 88800 Vittel for dates and hotel recommendations.

Slow food

La Foire aux Escargots takes place during the second week-end in May. Contact: Comité d'Animation, La Mairie, 88320

Martigny-les-Bains. (The nearest big towns are Contrexéville and Vittel.)

Undressing for lunch
Le Club 55, Plage de Pampelonne, 83350 Ramatuelle. Fax: 04.94.79.85.00. Lunch only. Dress optional.

Love at first sniff
La Foire aux Fromages at Livarot takes place during a week-end in early August. Contact: Office du Tourisme de Livarot, 1 Place G. Bisson, 14140 Livarot. (The nearest big town is Lisieux.)

A connoisseur's marathon
Le Marathon du Médoc takes place on a Saturday in mid-September. Contact: C.R.D Tourisme d'Aquitaine, Bureau de la Cité Mondiale, 23 Parvis des Chartrons, 33074 Bordeaux Cedex. Fax: 05.56.01.70.07.

Among flying corks in Burgundy
Les Trois Glorieuses are usually held during the third week-end in November, with the auction on the Sunday. Contact: C.R.D. Tourisme, Conseil Régional de Bourgogne, BP 1602, 21035 Dijon Cedex. Fax: 03.80.28.03.00.

Aristocrats with blue feet
Les Glorieuses normally take place during the last weekend before Christmas. Contact: Office du Tourisme, BP 190, Avenue Alsace Lorraine, 01000 Bourg-en-Bresse. L'Auberge

Bressane, 166 Boulevard de Brou. Fax: 04.74.23.03.15. Speciality: Bresse chicken.

The guided stomach
Hôtel d'Europe, 12 Place Crillon, 8400 Avignon. Fax: 04.90.14.76.71.

A civilized purge
Les Prés d'Eugénie, 40320 Eugénie les Bains. Fax: 05.58.51.10.10 (both for the hotel and the Domaine de Huchet on the beach).

Bon Appétit!
with

 &

Thank you for purchasing *Bon Appétit!* by Peter Mayle. To celebrate publication you are invited to start your own travels through the best of French cuisine, by taking part in our great 2 for 1 Café Rouge & Rouge offer. Visit any Café Rouge or Rouge, from August 1st 2001 to February 28th 2002 and when one person buys one main course, their guest gets *their* main course absolutely FREE!

The offer will run in all participating Café Rouge & Rouge restaurants listed over. Café Rouge & Rouge offer the perfect place to dine, relax and unwind in true French style.

To take up this offer please cut out the voucher printed below and present it at your chosen restaurant when arriving. See over for the full list of participating restaurants, together with the offer terms and conditions printed on the voucher below.

Bon Appétit!

BON APPÉTIT! 2 FOR 1 VOUCHER
This voucher entitles you to one FREE main course for your guest when you purchase any main course at participating Café Rouge or Rouge restaurant

OFFER TERMS AND CONDITIONS
- The voucher is valid when two people dine together at Café Rouge or Rouge
- Present this voucher at any Café Rouge or Rouge restaurant on arrival. Photocopied vouchers will not be accepted.
- The voucher will be exchanged for 1 free main course when another main course is purchased at full price (the cheaper main course of the 2 will be given for free).
- Only one main course may be claimed per voucher.
- The voucher is valid from August 1st 2001 until February 28th 2002 (excluding December 25th 2001, December 31st 2001, February 14th 2002).
- Offer is not valid with the Café Rouge & Rouge Xmas menu.
- This promotion is not valid in conjunction with any other offer or discount and there is no cash alternative.

AN AOL TIME WARNER COMPANY

Basingstoke 01256 334 556	Henley 01491 411733
Battersea 0207 924 3565	Hertford 01992 535353
Berkhamstead . . . 01442 878141	Highgate 0208 342 9797
Birmingham 0121 643 6556	Hitchin 01462 432962
Blackheath 0208 297 2727	James Street 0207 487 4847
Bournemouth . . . 01202 757472	Kingston Hill . . . 0208 547 3229
Brentwood 01277 262466	Kinghtsbridge . . . 0207 584 2345
Brighton 01273 774422	Lancer Square . . 0207 938 4200
Bromley 0208 460 0470	Leamington Spa . 01926 330565
Bury St Edmunds 01284 764477	Leeds 0113 245 1551
Cambridge 01223 364961	Loughton 0208 502 2011
Canary Wharf . . 0207 537 9696	Maida Vale 0207 286 2266
Chelmsford 01245 250588	Manchester 0161 839 0414
Cheltenham 01242 529989	Norwich 01603 624 230
Chichester 01243 781751	Nottingham 0115 958 2230
Chislehurst 0208 295 5000	Oxford 01865 310194
Chiswick 0208 742 7447	Pinner 0208 429 4424
Clapham 0208 673 3399	Plymouth 01752 665522
Didsbury 0161 438 0444	Putney 0208 788 4257
Dorking 01306 743400	Reigate 01737 223700
Dulwich 0208 7660070	Sheffield 0114 268 2232
Ealing 0208 579 2788	Shepherds Bush. . 0207 602 7732
Edinburgh 0131 225 4515	Solihull 0121 711 8881
Epsom 01372 749 131	Southgate 0208 886 3336
Esher 01372 465550	St Albans 01727 832777
Exeter 01392 211778	St Johns Wood . . 0207 722 8366
Farnham 01252 733688	St Pauls 0207 329 1234
Frith Street 0207 437 4307	Strand O/T Green 0208 995 6575
Gerrards Cross . . 01753 880601	Victoria 0207 931 9300
Greenwich 0208 293 6660	Wellington Street 0207 836 0998
Guildford 01483 451221	Weybridge 01932 851777
Hampstead 0207 435 4240	Whiteleys 0207 221 1509
Harrogate 01423 500043	Wimbledon 0208 944 5131
Hays Galleria . . . 0207 378 0097	Windsor 01753 831 100
Haywards Heath 01444 440888	York 01904 673293

For your nearest Rouge or Café Rouge click onto www.caferouge.co.uk

LIVAROT – Love at first sniff

MARTIGNY-LES-BAINS – Slow food

MÉDOC – A connoisseur's marathon

EUGÉNIE-LES-BAINS – A civilized purge

RICHERENCHES – For what we are about to receive

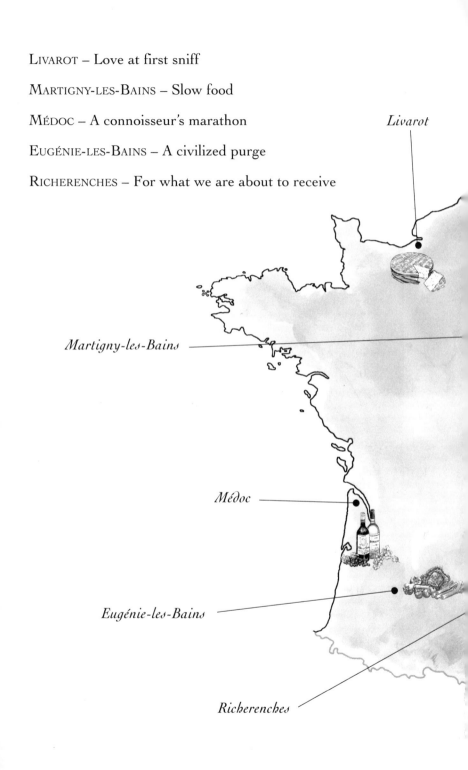

Livarot

Martigny-les-Bains

Médoc

Eugénie-les-Bains

Richerenches